Christianity, Society and Education

Robert Raikes, Past, Present and Future

Christianity, Society and Education

Robert Raikes, Past, Present and Future

Edited by
JOHN FERGUSON
President, Selly Oak Colleges, Birmingham

LONDON
SPCK

First published 1981
SPCK
Holy Trinity Church
Marylebone Road
London NW1 4DU

Printed in Great Britain at
The Camelot Press Ltd, Southampton

ISBN 0 281 03787 6

For
Canon David Paton

Who has done for the Bicentenary
what James Montgomery did for the
Golden Jubilee

Contents

Contents

Acknowledgements

Thanks are due to the following for permission to quote from copyright sources:

The Estate of Arnold Bennett and Associated Book Publishers Ltd: *Clayhanger* and *Anna of the Five Towns* by Arnold Bennett.

The National Christian Education Council: extracts from *The Sunday School Chronicle*.

Thanks are also due to Elnora Ferguson for compiling the index.

Introduction

The name Raikes is perhaps Danish. Robert Raikes's family came from Yorkshire: it is interesting to note that a seventeenth-century Raikes girl married a William Wilberforce. Robert himself was born in Gloucester in 1735. His mother was daughter of a cleric, his father the founder of the *Gloucester Journal*. His elder brother became a Director of the Bank of England. His nephew was a dandy, friend of Beau Brummell, and a diarist.

In 1757, not long out of his teens, and two years younger than the age at which Pitt was to become Prime Minister, he took over the editorship of the *Journal*. He was a conscientious editor, meticulous about facts. Not to him could be applied the words which Sheridan used of Mr Dundas: 'The Right Honourable gentleman is indebted to his memory for his jests, and to his imagination for his facts.' Not for him Mr Punch's biting comment on an editor:

> Upon his tomb let this inscription be–
> Comment to him was sacred, news was free.

'Matters of opinion', said Raikes, 'may not take place of matters of fact.' Humbert Wolfe wrote an epigram:

> You cannot hope to bribe or twist,
> Thank God, the British journalist.
> But, seeing what the man will do
> Unbribed, there's no occasion to.

Raikes had a contrary integrity as a journalist, and was fearless in exposing local abuses. He continued as editor till 1802, a period of forty-five years unremitting work.

Raikes was a great worker for prison reform: this is why it was particularly appropriate to ask Alan Baxendale, with his unrivalled knowledge, careful scholarship, and sound judgement, to contribute a paper on prison education to the present collection. In Raikes's day many were in prison for debt. But prison itself was corrupting. Raikes campaigned for the separate treatment of debtors, and himself paid off many debts from his own purse to secure the release of prisoners. Many prisoners were destitute. Tolerable conditions in prison depended on the prisoner's capacity to pay. As Raikes paid for the release of debtors, so he made contributions towards a more bearable incarceration for criminals. Even so conditions were promiscuous and insanitary. Raikes campaigned for improvement. In 1788 Fanny Burney was able to write:

> Every culprit is to have a separate cell. Every cell is clean, neat, and small, looking towards a wide expanse of country, and, far more fitted to his speculations, a rich expanse of the heavens. Air, cleanliness, and health seem all considered, but no other indulgence. The debtors also are considered, as they ought to be, with far more favour than the other offenders: and of course perfectly guarded from all intercourse with them.

It was a minor revolution.

But Raikes went beyond these palliatives, important as they might be. He tackled the causes of crime. What he had to say was amazingly and depressingly modern. The causes of crime in his view were primarily two. One was unemployment. 'If government or the magistrates of the country, seek not for some expedient of removing the plea of want of work, the excess of wickedness among the common people will destroy all the comforts to be levied from civil society.' Raikes saw the effects of the Industrial Revolution. He did not see the expropriation of labourers on the land, still less the rigidity of the Game Laws while men were starving. He saw the drift to the towns. He saw, and said, that retraining was essential. The other cause of crime was ignorance. 'Ignorance', he said, 'is generally the principal cause of these enormities.' The need to tackle unemployment and ignorance as two of the great causes of crime is still with us.

The Sunday school was in part Raikes's constructive answer to this last problem. As Frank Booth clearly shows, Raikes did not invent the Sunday school. Cardinal Borromeo, Joseph Alleine, Theophilus Lindsey, Hannah Ball and others had been there before him. Even in his own day the dissenting William King had set up an institution at Dursley, and Thomas Stock at Ashbury. Sir Harold Wilson did not *invent* the Open University: he seized the right moment to turn the dreams of others into his own reality. Raikes too seized the *kairos*, the right moment, the fullness of time. He did not invent the Sunday school. He initiated the Sunday-school movement.

His aim was complex. It was in part to dispel that ignorance which was a major cause of crime by offering education on the only day when children in full employment were free to receive it. It was in part to reduce the profanation of Sunday: cynics said that he was himself busily engaged on Sundays in marking up the newspaper for Monday and was constantly interrupted by the noise of the children. It was in part a genuine concern for children. Mrs Elliott ends her vivid account with the story of Raikes in old age recalling to Joseph Lancaster how he had been moved by the destitution of the children and the desecration of the Sabbath to cry 'Can nothing be done?' and heard a voice say 'Try'.

The first school began in Sooty Alley in 1780. It met from 10 to 12 and, after a break for lunch, met again from 1 to 5, a period which included a church service. The school had many merits – small classes, for example, and the use of student monitors. Raikes was interested in literacy, but he was still more interested in religious and moral instruction for which reading was an essential part. One of the historical 'spill-offs' from the evangelical Christian emphasis on the Bible was the literacy which it brought in its train. Raikes's very preoccupation with crime and its prevention tended to make the approach negative rather than positive. Raikes, as Shirley Elliott again notes, knew his Watts:

> For Satan finds some mischief still
> For idle hands to do.

The mother in *Punch* who says 'Go and see what Tommy's doing and tell him not to' is scarcely a caricature. The underlying attitude may be discerned in a phrase from a catechism in his Sunday Scholar's Companion: 'Conscience proves that there is a God, as a constable who serves us with a warrant proves there is a magistrate.' But, for all the limitations, Adam Smith said: 'No plan promised to effect a change of manners with equal ease and simplicity since the days of the Apostles.' The practical fruits were there. Mrs Elliott warns us not to overstate them. But in 1786 the Gloucester magistrates testified to the higher moral standards, and in July 1792 there were actually no cases at the Gloucester assizes.

Raikes met with opposition. Farm-owners thought that education would ruin agriculture. Rightists associated education for the poor with Tom Paine and the French Revolution. There were Christians who thought that the schools were destroying family religion; there were non-Christians or nominal Christians who proclaimed:

3

'Religion will neither fill our bellies nor clothe our bodies, and as to reading, it only serves to render poor folk proud and idle.'

But Raikes knew how to 'botanize with human nature'. In 1787 there were 201 schools with an enrolment of 10,232. Ten years later there were 1,086 schools with an enrolment of 69,000. In 1831, the year in which, somewhat oddly, the Golden Jubilee of the movement was celebrated through the energies of James Montgomery, whose hymnody was superior to his mathematics, the enrolment had risen to one-and-a-quarter million, and the number of teachers had topped the hundred thousand.

It is to celebrate, with a more accurate arithmetic than Montgomery's, the bicentenary of the movement that this collection of papers is offered. We have been fortunate to have the origins authoritatively re-presented. Lord Briggs, now Provost of Worcester College, Oxford, paints the background. He is a man who combines scholarship and charm in a rare degree, and who teaches nothing that he does not adorn. His association with the history of broadcasting, the journalism of the twentieth century, makes him a particularly appropriate opening batsman. Frank Booth and Shirley Elliott, both from Raikes's county of Gloucestershire, have been engaged in fresh research on Raikes and his career; Frank Booth has written a new biography which will replace his worthy but not entirely satisfactory predecessors in the field.

From Raikes himself we move to what many regard as the great era of the Sunday school, the nineteenth century. Dr Malcolm Dick, in his carefully researched paper, concentrates upon what was happening in Stockport in the first fifty years of the movement. Colin Riches of the Open University offers an unusual view of the impact of the Sunday school in the nineteenth century through the evidence of literature. Finally in this section Gerald Knoff, the distinguished historian of the World Sunday-school Movement, traces that movement with a vitality which matches its own, and takes us into the twentieth century. The 'yells' of the American delegates are only one pen-picture bringing the scene vividly to life.

It has been the clear purpose of all of us associated with the bicentenary that it should not be an exercise in nostalgia, but should be strongly related to the present and the future. The Revd Krister Ottosson, who is concerned with educational work in the Diocese of Durham, and was formerly Education Secretary with the British Council of Churches, raises important questions about the interaction of education and society: this is indeed a challenging exercise in Christian basics. More of this in a moment.

Next the Revd Philip Cliff, Head of Church Education at Westhill College, himself a leading expert on Raikes, provides a link with the second section in carrying the story of the Sunday school on to the present day, with an admirable appraisal of the work of G. H. Archibald and H. A. Hamilton, both of whom were in fact closely linked with Westhill. Alan Baxendale then offers a link with another of Raikes's concerns, conditions in prisons, with his careful, factual, concerned, but unemotional account of what has been and what can be achieved in prison education. There is an emphasis here upon patience and realism, but also upon dedication and hope. Certainly those of us who have worked with the Open University know how meaningful educational opportunities are to long-term prisoners, a window on the world, a ray of hope. One of the most moving letters I have ever received came from a tutor to one of these prison groups. She wanted to tell me how much my units on Socrates had meant to the prisoners, who identified themselves with Socrates in prison, but at the same time saw that he had something which they lacked and would like to have. She told me too of the seminar she organized when the governor allowed a group of tutorial students to come in from outside. The prisoners were nervous and shy, but when they found that they could hold their own in discussion with the others it helped to reinforce their new sense of positive purpose. Recently I have been in correspondence with a prisoner who on graduating wishes to master medieval Latin and go on to research on a medieval theological treatise. The prisons have been called universities of crime. They will be that less, the more we can offer constructive and purposive education of another kind. It is part of a process of reclamation, or, if you will, of redirection.

Next we ask some questions about the churches' mission to children. We in Britain have become uncomfortably aware that the schools have been doing much of our work for us. A quarter of a century ago – I am speaking from memory – a survey was carried out in Britain and America. Two key questions were 'Are you a church member?' and 'Name the four Gospels'. Church membership in the U.S.A. was of the order of 90 per cent: in Britain it was more like 15 per cent. Yet in Britain 50 per cent of those questioned could name all four Gospels and in the U.S.A. 50 per cent could not name even one. The difference of course lay in the provision in the state schools. To name the Gospels is not the be-all and end-all of Christian education, but even so the discrepancy is startling. Britain has now become a multi-faith community, and in many educational authorities the provision for religious education recognizes this. In the early 1970s I chaired a multi-faith conference (including the humanists) at Leicester on religious education. We were unanimous in saying that religious education is an essential part of education, that it consists not in dogmatic indoctrination into any one religion but in helping the growing children to have an understanding awareness of the religious dimension of life and the existence of religions, and to find their own life-styles. No doubt in a country of primarily Christian tradition, religious education in schools will continue to focus attention on Christianity. But there will be less than before of an exclusive concentration on Christianity; knowledge of the Bible will inevitably be less thorough. There are many grown people, with a reputable education behind them, and lively and curious minds, who would be as hard put to explain

> Of man's first disobedience and the fruit
> Of that forbidden tree, whose mortal taste
> Brought death into the world, and all our woe,
> With loss of Eden, till one greater Man
> Restore us, and regain the blissful seat,
> Sing, heav'nly Muse.

as

> Those other two equall'd with me in fate
> So were I equall'd with them in renown,
> Blind Thamyris and blind Maeonides,
> And Tiresias and Phineus, prophets old.

The churches will have to look to their laurels.

Here Kathryn Copsey of the Newham Community Renewal Scheme takes a hard look at the problems of children in the inner city. David Sheppard's *Built as a City* is the finest appraisal of inner-city problems and opportunities I have ever read, but Kathryn Copsey provides a remarkable miniature of the child in that environment. What she has to say about the failure of the churches to achieve any real integration between adults and children is clearly true and deeply disturbing. The churches' failure in integration has to do with age as well as race. We Christians do well to remember that in breaking fellowship with a child we are breaking fellowship with the Lord. For if any who receives one of these little ones receives him, it must be true that any who fails to receive one of these little ones fails to receive him.

John H. Westerhoff III of Duke University Divinity School also takes off from the theme of nurture. Prof. Westerhoff might not himself say so, but the American churches are light-years ahead of the British churches in their provision for education within church life. His emphasis on the reintegration of kerygma and didache is important both theologically and practically, and the truths he propounds extend far beyond the horizon of the United States. His opening gambit from Augustine, that time is a threefold present, the present as we experience it, the past as present memory, and the future as present expectation, expresses well the basis on which this whole symposium is planned, looking from the past through the present to the future.

'Education and Society'. It is a great subject. Is education an oilcan to keep the wheels of society turning, or is it a spanner to throw into the works? Education is itself a present bridge between the past and the future. But which world is it to reflect? There is no doubt that the conscious direction of education has been mainly towards conserving and reinforcing the values of existing society. So Eric Havelock, in an immensely stimulating analysis of Ancient Greece, suggests that what Plato calls the quarrel between poets and philosophers existed precisely because the poets were the repositories of accepted social wisdom, and were the staple fare of education, and the philosophers were challenging both. So the classical Chinese universities were offering efficient administration to stabilize the order of society, the medieval universities were producing the clerisy, the liberal university of Newman and Jowett was offering an education appropriate to the British ruling-class and its products went out to govern vast tracts of Asia or Africa with Sophocles or Thucydides or Cicero or Horace in their pockets, the American university of the mid-twentieth century showed what Abraham Flexner scathingly called a 'service-station mentality', helping (as he put it) 'third-rate book-keepers to become second-rate book-keepers' and helping to perpetuate the common beliefs on which American society rested.

But this is not the whole story. An oilcan can be thrown into the works, just as a spanner can be used to secure the wheels of society. A wise man once said 'Education is like ivory. You grab hold of a chunk of it and find that attached to it is a whopping great beast that you don't know what to do with!' So the education designed to preserve Athenian democratic values produced Plato, who challenged them. Plato's Academy produced the renegade Aristotle. The liberal German university produced Karl Marx. And Clark Kerr's Berkeley produced Mario Savio. The tragedy, though perhaps also the safeguard, is that those who seek to change society are conditioned by the very society they seek to change. As Harold Loukes said, 'even when they rebel, even rebel radically, they rebel with the language and moral concepts and social tools they have learned in that society'.

As Christians we have a special insight to offer. Henri Bergson made the distinction between the Closed Society and the Open Society. They differ *toto caelo*, and when we look at their moralities we can see at once where we as Christians stand. The morality of the closed society is legalistic, easily to be pinpointed, inflexible. The morality of the Open Society is personal, open, hard to catch within the pincers of a rule. They stand as law to love, as the Torah to the Sermon on the Mount. If we really believe in a living God, in a Father who is still at work, in a God who is love, if we believe that Jesus is he who makes all things new, if, with John Robinson, pastor to the Pilgrim Fathers, we accept that 'the Lord hath yet more light and truth to break forth from his holy word', we cannot uphold a closed society or a closed system of education. 'These are they that have turned the world upside down' was how they spoke of the first apostles. A nun, who as a student sang in one of my madrigal groups, later sent us a banner: 'Faith leads to adventure.'

This has consequences for education. Of course there is a properly conservative element within any educational system. Society may or may not need book-keepers, but it certainly needs doctors and engineers, and if there are to be book-keepers they had better be second-rate than third-rate. There is also a properly open-ended and, in its consequences, revolutionary element in the sort of education which the Christian will be concerned to offer, and if in the nature of what we are saying, we cannot offer a rigid structure, we can offer some directions. We can foster attitudes of co-operation; we might even do more to encourage teamwork among teachers: as staff of the Open University can testify, it is time-consuming, traumatic, frustrating, exciting, and rewarding. We can encourage 'conscientization', to use the ugly but powerful word which the

Latin American educators have devised. Above all we must not be afraid of change. We must indeed challenge the sort of rigidity in an educational system which does not admit change, experiment, variety. Education for the Open Society must be flexible. Tolstoy once said that 'the only method of education is experiment, and its only criterion freedom'.

Take one area where there is powerful current concern, education for peace. From the banning of the sale of war-toys in Sweden to the School of Peace Studies in the University of Bradford there are fascinating explorations in progress. Yet as soon as we begin to be involved we realize how little we know. We cannot even define peace. Within the School of Peace Studies at Bradford both among teachers and learners there are those who espouse absolute pacifism, and neo-Marxists who believe that peace can be attained only if an unjust order of society is overthrown, by violence if necessary. Even a Christian pacifist may say (with Dick Sheppard) that he stands not for peace at any price but for love at all costs. We do not know whether war-toys and 'Cowboys and Indians' help to perpetuate attitudes of violence or to work them out of the system. We do not know whether, with the rejection of age by youth, militant parents and teachers or pacifistic parents and teachers are more likely to produce peaceable offspring. We do not know whether 'ritualized aggression' in games and other fields is desirable or dangerous. We do not know whether team-games make for peace or (as Illich suggests) a more intensive competitiveness. We do not know whether encouraging a person to be a good loser is training in constructive attitudes or reinforcing the power structures of society. And if (as some educators hold) education for peace must mean a refusal of the teacher to impose himself, then the outcome must be totally uncertain.

But we can, as the result of practical experience, draw some conclusions. We can firmly say that training to kill is wrong. We can deprecate history textbooks which inculcate nationalistic attitudes or give a romantic glorification of war rather than a realistic account of it: Michael Grant once said that Caesar was the most insidiously dangerous author to put in the hands of beginners in Latin, because he was a subtle propagandist for his own militarism and dictatorship. We can assert that corporal punishment should be used only as a last resort. Positively, we can develop the value of co-operation. We can and should institute training in non-violence; even those

Christians who accept violence as a regrettable necessity in the last resort, maintain that it is permissible only when non-violent methods have been explored to the full, and this is scarcely possible without some prior training. We can show a personal concern for individuals which cuts across the sort of 'group-labelling' which reinforces violent attitudes. (The American Principal who said to a boy, of neat appearance and courteous manner, who was also a dance-band leader, 'if I let you grow your hair long, I'd be treating you as an individual', may have had a problem, but it was not entirely outside himself.) We can ourselves show the attitudes appropriate to the Open Society, which, because it 'is the society which is deemed in principle to embrace all humanity', is ultimately incompatible with war. All this would be to challenge the accepted *mores* of society in the name of values to which the majority give verbal assent.

Raikes would not have spoken of the Open Society. But he believed strongly in the moral and religious impact of education on the individual and so on society. He did not disown the practical aspects of it either. Hence the insistence, though it was less evident in the Sunday-school curriculum, on the importance of retraining. Here is the paradoxical richness of what a healthy education must offer. It must be a preparation for work: education has always had a properly vocational aspect, though it is liable to become a strait-jacket if it becomes too narrowly vocational. It must also be a preparation for leisure, not least in a world in which a rational economy will soon provide the four-day and even the three-day week and an irrational one will leave two or three million unemployed (in Britain). It is concerned with the individual. It is also concerned with the community; to be taught in isolation is doubtfully to be called an education at all. It is directed to conserving values. It is directed to developing minds which will challenge falsely accepted values. In the old antithesis, like Ezekiel, it exercises the functions of both priest and prophet.

So Raikes still speaks to us today, speaks to us as a Christian, as a reformer, as one concerned with the poor and needy, as one concerned with children, as an educator, as one of those makers of history who produce an idea bigger than himself. Our conditions are not identical with his. But in our own days and our own ways his questions still press forward. First, how shall we meet the challenges of unemployment, crime, purposeless drifting, and senseless violence? Second, what have we as Christians to do to help those who are in desperate need through no fault of their own? Third, how can education serve to meet these challenges? Fourth, what can the churches do to provide education in Christian living?

John Westerhoff ends on a note of optimism sounded by the most profoundly optimistic of Victorian poets, Browning, at the outset of 'Rabbi Ben Ezra':

> Grow old along with me!
> The best is yet to be,
> The last of life, for which the first was made:
> Our times are in His hand
> Who saith, 'A whole I planned,
> Youth shows but half; trust God; see all nor be afraid!'

Education is about wholeness. It is about loving God (and loving our fellow-men, without which it is not possible that we love God) with heart and soul and mind and strength. Education for wholeness is education for peace; *shalom*, the Hebrew word we translate 'peace', comes from a root meaning 'wholeness'. So we say with the other great Victorian prophet-poet Tennyson,

> Let knowledge grow from more to more,
> But more of reverence in us dwell,
> The mind and soul according well
> May make one music as before,

> But vaster.

But vaster.

JOHN FERGUSON
Selly Oak Colleges
Birmingham

Part I

Raikes and his Age

Innovation and Adaptation:
the Eighteenth-Century Setting

Asa Briggs

There was no shortage of criticism in late-eighteenth-century England. Dr John Brown's *An Estimate of the Manners and Principles of the Times*, published in 1757, soon ran into seven editions. Fourteen years later, a more persuasive writer, Horace Walpole, described England as 'a gaming, wrangling, railing nation without principles, genius, character or allies'.

The critics did not agree about what was wrong. Many of them felt, like Dr Johnson, that there was too much 'innovation', often associated with 'insubordination'. Others felt old ways needed to be 'improved' and that the difficulties of society began at the top, not at the bottom. Some welcomed 'enthusiasm', others feared and attacked it. There were even sharp differences of opinion on 'education'. Some saw it as the hope of the future. Others mistrusted its likely consequences. 'If a horse knew as much as a man,' Mandeville had written in his *Essay on Charity and Charity Schools* in 1723, 'I should not like to be his rider.' By contrast Adam Smith in his influential *Wealth of Nations* (1776) argued that the more 'the inferior ranks of the people' were educated, the less liable they would be to 'the delusions of enthusiasm and superstition, which, among ignorant nations, frequently occasion the most dreadful disorders'.

Charity schools were the favourite early-eighteenth-century response to the education of 'the inferior ranks'. By 1730 there were nearly 1,500 of them, teaching over 22,000 pupils. The Society for Promoting Christian Knowledge, founded in 1698, did much to sponsor the idea which in Richard Steele's phrase represented one of the 'greatest instances of public spirit the age had produced'. The intensity of the effort to found and to maintain charity schools reflected both concern and interest, a characteristic eighteenth-century philanthropic combination. Bishop Butler, who understood the combination perfectly, stressed that the aim of the charity schools was

> not in any sort to remove poor children out of the rank in which they were born, but, keeping them in it, to give them the assistance

15

which their circumstances plainly called for, by educating them in the principles of religion as well as of civil life.

Nor did the Puritan dissenter, Isaac Watts, disagree:

> I would persuade myself that the masters and mistresses of these schools among us teach the children of the poor which are under their care to know what their station in life is, how mean their circumstances, how necessary 'tis for them to be diligent, laborious, honest and faithful, humble and submissive, what duties they owe the rest of mankind and particularly to their superiors.

'To avoid all Quarrelling and Contention' was the ninth rule to be observed by the children at one representative charity school in the Midlands, and an advertisement for a schoolmaster's post in the North explained that it was 'requisite and necessary' that charity school children should be 'inured to some easy labour . . . for the promoting Industry in our extensive Manufacture'. The Westminster Charity School *Minute Book* in the metropolis looked outside the workshop to the community. Uneducated children contracted 'Evil Customs and Habits' which became 'the Curse and Trouble of all places where they live' and often 'by their Wicked Actions' were 'brought to Shameful and Untimely Death'.

The view from below could be different, and as the century went by the sense of 'station' was often accepted less meekly. Adam Smith was not alone in directing attention to 'the natural effort of every individual to better his own condition'. John Millar in his *Origin of the Distinction of Ranks in Society* (1771) urged that 'every man who is industrious may entertain the hope of gaining a fortune'. The old conception of 'industry' was changing in a society which became more 'industrial', a new term. The entrepreneur was expected to be enterprising as well as diligent. Out of such expectations new gospels of self-help were forged. Of course, as industry began to acquire new forms of visible expression – in forges, factories, and warehouses – the need to persuade those working for wages in the new units of production and distribution to work hard and honestly strengthened rather than diminished. The rhythms of work were altering just as was the social and cultural context of the new industrial town. Factories required 'rules' just as much as charity schools had done: so, too, did the towns themselves. But the 'best' workers and citizens were those who did not need external sanctions to make

16

them work hard and live well. The most effective discipline came from within.

Eighteenth-century experience, including changing experience, must be taken into account in any study of the emergence and development of Sunday schools, and three aspects of late-eighteenth-century experience are particularly relevant. First, population was growing, stimulating a vigorous debate on its causes and consequences and posing almost every kind of urban problem – health, public order, administration. The first decennial census was taken in 1801 – an earlier attempt to introduce one had been turned down by Parliament in 1735 – but long before then the trends were clear – more towns, bigger towns, a change in the weight of population from the South and East to the North and West. W. Thompson in his *Tour of England and Scotland* (1788) described the growth of cities like Birmingham: 'about fifty years ago, there were only three principal or leading streets in Birmingham, which at this day is so crowded, and at the same time so extensive a town.' And Horace Walpole put it even more dramatically three years later: 'There will soon be one street from London to Brentford; ay, and from London to every village ten miles around . . . Nor is there any depopulation from the country . . . Birmingham, Manchester, Hull and Liverpool would serve any king in Europe for a capital, and would make the Empress of Russia's mouth water.'

Second, awareness that growth posed problems directed special attention to the position of children. 'Great towns are in a peculiar degree fatal to children', wrote Thomas Percival of Manchester in 1775. 'Half of all that are born in London die under three, and in Manchester under five years of age.' The survivors were often thought of as 'wild running' and in need of discipline. 'He who plays as a boy will play as a man' said Wesley in one of his least attractive aphorisms, far removed in feeling from his contemporary Rousseau. Wesley's mother had been equally strict: she believed in 'breaking the wills' of children. Of her own children she wrote 'when turned a year old (and some before) they were taught to fear the rod, and to cry softly'. It is agreeable to turn in contrast to the Nonconformist minister Philip Doddridge who stressed the importance of tenderness and patience in dealing with children: 'do not desire to terrify or amaze them, to lead them into unnecessary severities, or to deprive them of innocent pleasures.'

Third, there was a preoccupation with crime – its causes and consequences and the best way of dealing with it. The preoccupation was associated with an interest in the theory and practice of punishment. The Salford magistrates passed a long resolution at their August Quarter Sessions in 1786 very specifically relating the growth of Sunday schools to crime control, noting how 'idle, disorderly and dangerous persons of all descriptions' were wandering around and that 'where Sunday schools have been opened, their good effects have been plainly perceived in the orderly and decent Comportment of the Youth who are instructed therein'. 'If these Institutions should become established throughout the Kingdom,' the magistrates went on, 'there is good reason to hope that they will produce a happy change in the general Morals of the People, and thereby render the Severities of Justice less frequently necessary.' It is interesting to note that Robert Raikes, who was keenly interested in prison reform, believed that the sight of a prison would deter wrongdoers. 'Could unhappy wretches see the misery that awaits them in a crowded gaol they would surely relinquish the gratifications that reduce them to such a state of wretchedness.' Not far away from Raikes's Gloucester a Guardian Society for the Prosecution of Felons, Forgers, Receivers of Stolen Goods, etc., was set up at Bath during the 1780s. Voluntary action was deemed to be necessary, and the Society was hailed as a 'laudable Undertaking, the good effects of which have been sensibly felt by the Public'.

Paradoxically Sunday was a day of crime. 'Farmers and other inhabitants of the towns and villages', Raikes wrote in the *Gloucester Journal* in 1783, 'complain that they receive more injury to their property on the Sabbath than all the week besides: this, in a great measure, proceeds from the lawless state of the younger class, who are allowed to run wild on that day, free from every restraint.' The *Manchester Mercury* took up the same theme a year later. 'The hardest Heart must melt at the melancholy Sight of such a Multitude of Children, both Male and Female, in this Town, who live in gross Ignorance, Infidelity and habitual Profanation of the Lord's Day. What crowds fill the Streets! tempting each other to Idleness, Play, Lewdness, and every other Species of Wickedness . . . To attempt a remedy is laudable and divine.' After Sunday schools had been introduced, Bishop Porteus of Chester could write in 1785 that they were particularly necessary in 'such populous manufacturing towns as Manchester, where the children are during the weekdays generally employed in work and on the Sundays are too apt to be idle, mischievous and vicious.'

The introduction of Sunday schools in the 1780s was not accidental, therefore. This was a decade, indeed, when 'innovation' was in the air. The steam engine was the main symbol of progress and its economic results were already manifest. Production indices soared, whole landscapes changed their appearance, expectations were changing. 'Move your eye which side you will,' wrote Arthur Young, 'you behold nothing but greater riches and yet greater resources.' The economic gains more than compensated for the loss of the American colonies, recognized by treaty in 1783. In the same year Dr Johnson proclaimed that 'the age is mad after innovation' although it should be added that his was a complaint and that it was inspired by the abolition of the procession to the scaffolds at Tyburn, a popular entertainment in the eighteenth century, and the introduction of the drop to hasten death by hanging. Another innovation of a year later – John Palmer's use of stage coaches to carry mail – was introduced not far from Raikes's Gloucester at Bath. There was almost as much argument as to whether Raikes really had invented Sunday schools as there was about Richard Arkwright's inventions, and there was the same kind of rapture on one side and mistrust on the other. 'The improvement of these children in learning has been wonderful,' wrote a Manchester pamphleteer in 1785, 'and when they sing to the praise and glory of their maker, they appear a tribe of embryo-angels training for the skies. Every Christian heart glows with triumph; and heaven seems for a moment transplanted upon earth.' Yet a Stockport clergyman maintained that the 'modern Sunday school' – and 'modern' was a pejorative adjective – violated the Sabbath when 'any kind of learning is taught during the season of public worship and made to serve instead of it, and where any instructions are given, on any part of the day, which relate to this world and not immediately to the soul'.

Whatever the reactions Raikes was as successful as Arkwright in establishing a 'system'. Gloucester was far away from the new industrial districts, but soon Sunday schools established themselves there. John Wesley noted in the West Riding, for example, that Sunday schools were 'springing up wherever he went', and a Birmingham advertisement drew attention to the fact that 'the utility of these Seminaries for the instruction of the lower class of the people [note that the word 'class' was just coming into fashion in place of the older terms 'rank', 'degree', and 'station'] and a due observance of the Sabbath' had been 'proved in different parts of England'. 'A well wisher to such a laudable institution,' the advertisement went on, 'requests the inhabitants of Birmingham to meet on that business . . . on Wednesday morning, the 7th instant, at ten o'clock precisely.'

It was not long before the Sunday-school system became more general than the factory system, although there were some areas of the country where it was far stronger than in others. In the rural areas there was often the sharpest opposition. M. G. Jones, author of the standard history of charity schools, has described in her biography of Hannah More how Hannah battled to establish Sunday schools in the Mendips where there were parishes with 'as much knowledge of Christ as in the interior of Africa'. Religion, some farmers stated, would ruin agriculture: Sunday schools, some clergy stated, would ruin religion. There was more of a tradition of philanthropy in the old towns and more drive to create new institutions through voluntary action. The *Manchester Mercury*, one of an increasing number of vigorous opinion-forming provincial journals, printed 'An Address to the Public on Sunday Schools' in August 1784 in which it was urged that the neglect of education was a principal cause of 'the Misery of Families, Cities and Nations: Ignorance, Vice and Misery, being constant Companions.' Hannah More, who shared the same values as the writer, was struck above all else in the rural districts by the poverty: 'I believe I see more misery in a week than some people believe exists in the whole world.' Both she and the writer believed that 'the grand object of instruction' was the Bible: both believed that it was reading rather than writing that mattered most.

Four points must be made by the general historian about the spread of the Sunday-school *movement* – as it quickly came to be conceived – between the 1780s and the end of the Napoleonic Wars in 1815. First, it cannot be treated in isolation from other events and processes. The Proclamation Society, founded in 1787, advocated a 'reformation in manners'. Vice and immorality were defined to include neglect of Sabbath observance, drunkenness, blasphemy, the keeping of gaming houses, and the sale of indecent or licentious publications. The Society, which was in line of descent from the Society for the Reformation of Manners, founded in 1692, conceived of itself as 'censor of the religion and morals of the country'. It was willing to enlist the aid of legislation to protect or to raise moral standards, yet it drew on the strength of mobilized opinion.

Second, mobilized opinion included aristocratic opinion. Hannah More worked with the poor, but she drew much of her support from the rich. 'Tell her to live in the world,' John Wesley is reputed to have said to her, 'there is the sphere of her usefulness; they will not let us come nigh them.' Two of her most effective volumes were *Thoughts on the Importance of the Manners of the Great to General Society* and *Estimate of the Religion of the Fashionable World*. T. H. White has called his little book on this period *The Age of Scandal* (1950). It was increasingly an age, however, with two faces. 'Nothing can be a greater contrast than my life here and that I usually lead,' wrote Lady Bessborough to her lover on a visit to her family's home in 1797.

As the clock strikes eight I am down at Prayers, then breakfast, then I give Caroline her lessons as usual, read or write for a while till my Mother send for me to help her in teaching her School Girls. I acquit myself *tant bien que mal*, and often wonder what you . . . would say to see me stuck up in the midst of an old ruin'd Abbey teaching some little Beggar Girls to spell and sing. We dine at three, are out all evening after tea, return generally to have some music, in which the Chaplain's wife particularly shines . . . At nine ye bell rings for Prayers, then supper, and at ten not a mouse is stirring in the whole House. I hope you are edified with the length of my letter and the importance of its contents.

Third, edification often went with 'vital religion', whether that religion were Anglican – and this was the form which it most often took with the aristocracy – or Methodist – and this was the form which it most often took with the poor. (The middle classes, who included a sizeable number of old Dissenters, may well have found it easier to behave than the very rich or the very poor, for as a writer in the *Monthly Review* put it in 1807 'mediocrity of station' was favourable to 'domestic virtue'.) There was a certain ecumenicism in the early stages of religious revival, and it can be traced in the history of Sunday schools also. In Manchester, for instance, Anglicans and Dissenters worked well together at first, though the former distributed the Prayer Book and the latter Isaac Watts's *Divine Songs for*

Children. Likewise the London-based Society for the Support and Encouragement of Sunday Schools, founded in 1785, was sponsored by a Baptist merchant but governed by a council of twelve Anglicans and twelve Dissenters 'united to prevent the corruption of morals and advance the peace and felicity of the country'. Some Evangelicals remained a little unhappy about the 'work' element in the Sunday schools. 'Resolved that no teacher shall be permitted to instruct any children belonging to the Sunday schools in writing on the Lord's Day' read a minute of the Manchester Sunday School Society in 1786. For many reasons writing, as distinct from reading, always provoked controversy.

Fourth, the social as distinct from the educational (and even the religious) aspects of 'improvement' were always stressed. The Society for the Support and Encouragement of Sunday Schools had among its objectives

> to prevent vice – to encourage industry and virtue – to dispel the darkness of ignorance – to diffuse the light of knowledge – to bring men cheerfully to submit to their stations – to obey the laws of God and their country – to make that part of the community, the country poor, happy – to lead them in the pleasant paths of religion here, and to endeavour to prepare them for a glorious eternity.

This was more appropriate language for rural areas and for small towns than for industrial areas, although the phrase 'to obey the laws of God and country' acquired new point in those areas and elsewhere after the French Revolution and the outbreak of the long wars against revolutionary France in 1793. The alliance between Nonconformists and Anglicans often broke down during the 1790s even in relation to the organization of Sunday schools, since the Nonconformists included sympathizers with the Revolution and the Anglicans intolerant bigots who smelled revolutionaries everywhere. The Manchester Sunday School Committee in 1793 demanded the dismissal of 'any teacher or assistant who shall be proved to be disaffected to the present Government'. Meanwhile, Hannah More was writing cheap anti-revolutionary tracts which have been variously described as 'antidotes to Tom Paine' – a contemporary description – and 'Burke for beginners'.

Once again, this was only one side of a complicated issue. William Godwin, the influential anarchist writer, argued in his *Enquiry Concerning Political Justice* (1797) that 'the chief lessons' taught in Sunday school were 'a superstitious veneration for the Church of England and to bow to every man in a handsome coat'. None the less, the radical Samuel Bamford noted at the end of the Napoleonic wars how 'the Sunday schools of the preceding thirty years had produced many working men of sufficient talent to become readers, writers and speakers in the village meetings for Parliamentary reform'. Likewise, a different kind of Lancashire radical, Archibald Prentice, observed that Sunday-school teachers 'with the single undeviating purpose of promoting the eternal welfare of their pupils' were in fact 'preparing them for the fit discharge of their social and public duties. They were creating thought among the hitherto unthinking masses.'

Prentice was writing in 1851, and by then there were secular as well as Christian Sunday schools – some of them were very famous in Lancashire – and Robert Owen had taken over Raikes's message. The nineteenth-century story was one of adaptation as well as of growth. For A. P. Wadsworth, twentieth-century editor of the *Manchester Guardian* and one of the first historians to write about the subject in a scholarly way, Sunday schools 'were begun as a form of police precaution imposed from above, and imbued with authoritarianism. They were transformed by the genius of ordinary people into a vital part of a democratic society.' They were a 'miserable substitute for day schooling'. Yet they 'formed a point of social contact in a confused and shifting community' and 'encouraged that spirit of voluntary service and voluntary organization which is, perhaps, almost the best thing the nineteenth century bequeathed to us'. Wadsworth's view of the 'police' function is rather too restricted, and he did not note how the eighteenth century passed on to the nineteenth its own legacy of voluntarism. His emphasis on 'the genius of ordinary people' has been echoed, however, by the most recent historian of Sunday schools, the American historian T. W. Laqueur, in his book *Religion and Respectability: Sunday Schools and Working Class Culture 1780–1850*.

Historians, by concentrating their efforts on a few large schools, two London-based Sunday school societies, and a handful of prominent Evangelicals, have obscured the part played by men and women of the 'lower orders' in improving the lot of their children . . . The fact that local sources reveal so large a number of hitherto forgotten names suggests that the Sunday school from its earliest days was to a large extent a product of the working-class community. Education and improvement were not the monopoly of latter day Puritans from the middling orders of society.

It is useful to set alongside Lady Bessborough's comments the remarks of Bamford about his old Methodist Sunday school which was open every Sunday morning at half-past eight

for the instruction of whatever child crossed its threshold. A hymn was first read out and sung by the scholars and teachers. An extempore prayer followed, all the scholars and teachers kneeling at their places; the classes ranging from those of the spelling book to those of the Bible, then commenced their lessons, girls in the gallery above, and boys below. Desks which could either be moved up or down, like the leaf of a table, were arranged all round the school, against the walls of the gallery, as well as against those below, and at measured distances the walls were numbered. Whilst the Bible and Testament classes were reading their first lesson, the desks were got ready, inkstands and copy-books numbered, containing copies and pens, were placed opposite corresponding numbers on the wall; and when the lesson was concluded the writers took their places, each at his own number, and so continued their instruction. When the copy was finished, the book was shut and left on the desk, a lesson of spelling was gone through, and at twelve o'clock singing and prayer again took place, and the scholars were dismissed. At one o'clock there was service in the chapel, and soon after two the school re-assembled, girls now occupying the writing desks, as boys had done in the forenoon, and at four or half-past the scholars were sent home for the week.

It is a memorable picture and it catches the spirit of the struggle for literacy, a struggle which was as specific to that time as the watching of television is today. There are other pictures which linger.

The spiritual improvement of the parish [a theme deliberately left out by Wadsworth] was left entirely to the care and management of Tommy Jones and Johnny Hart . . . but a Higher Power not only presided over, but greatly blessed these two poor youths, who are concealed from all human sight in the bowels of the earth six days out of seven, and on the seventh day they emerge, like two young apostles, to instruct and enlighten the rising generation.

Robert Raikes:
Founder of the Sunday-School Movement

Frank Booth

The advent of the Sunday-school movement had far-reaching effects on the religious and social life of this country. Eighteenth-century Sunday schools were not only a social disciplinary force saving untold numbers of the common people from punishment under the cruel laws of the land, but an institution which strongly, and beneficially, influenced relationships within communities. Through the establishment of Sunday school many clergymen actively undertook the Church's holy trust – the care of the poor. The well-to-do saw in the Sunday school a worth-while charity, advantageous to their own interests. The rapid development of the Sunday-school movement, thanks in no small measure to Robert Raikes, the printer of Gloucester, was incredible and the power of education was brought by thousands to hundreds of thousands.

The date of greatest significance in the beginning of the Sunday-school movement was perhaps 3 November 1783. On that day Raikes included the following (now famous) paragraph in his newspaper, the *Gloucester Journal*:

Some of the clergy in different parts of the country bent upon attempting a reform among the children of the lower class, are establishing Sunday Schools, for the rendering of the Lord's day subservient to the ends of instruction, which has hitherto been prostituted to bad purposes. Farmers, and other inhabitants of towns and villages, complain they receive more injury in their property on the Sabbath, than all the week besides: This in a great measure proceeds from the lawless state of the younger class, who are allowed to run wild, on that day, free from any restraint. To remedy this evil, persons duly qualified are employed to instruct those that may have learned to read, are taught the catechism, and conducted to church. By thus keeping their minds engaged, the day passes profitably, and not disagreeably. In those parishes where this plan has been adopted, we are assured, that the behaviour of the children is greatly civilized. The

25

barbarous ignorance, in which they had before lived, being in some degree dispelled; they begin to give proofs that those persons are mistaken, who consider the lower orders of mankind as incapable of improvement, and therefore think an attempt to reclaim them impracticable, or at least not worth the trouble.

Small wonder that the paragraph was copied in the London newspapers. Raikes had answered in the affirmative two questions long to be debated in eighteenth- and nineteenth-century England: could and should the children of the poor be educated? The depravity, immorality, disorderliness, and brutality of the 'lower orders' was a problem of constant concern to the propertied classes. Raikes offered a solution: the effectiveness of Sunday-school instruction in improving the behaviour of the poor he reported as proven. Raikes's argument proved convincing and had wide appeal. Reference to farmers was most pertinent, the country being chiefly agricultural. People in towns also were confronted, particularly on Sundays, with offensive and unruly behaviour by children of the poor. Authorities were concerned about the increase in crime and the youthfulness of the offenders. Worth noting too is that the initiative for setting up Sunday schools was attributed to the clergy, and this in an age when the clergy too frequently neglected the duties of their office and religious conviction was often a subject for ridicule.

Raikes, a skilful journalist, was uniquely situated to give publicity to the work of the Sunday schools. He had the motivation, conviction, determination, personality, and the means. As the owner of 'one of the two greatest provincial newspapers' with an extensive circulation, he had control of part of the most effective media of the day.

Raikes wrote from experience, having personally observed changes for the better in children's behaviour as a result of their attendance at Sunday School. In 1780, with his friend and co-worker, the Revd Thomas Stock, Curate of St John's Church, Gloucester, he had founded Sunday schools in that city. For three years before he made his notable announcement, he had been visiting the homes of poor parents persuading them to send their children to Sunday school, and had been helping to teach youngsters, who on former Sundays, when the factories were closed, were left to their own devices.

Raikes, was not, of course, the founder of the first Sunday school. Charles Borromeo, Archbishop of Milan, established Sunday schools there in the sixteenth century and three men in the seventeenth century, Joseph Woodward, a Puritan Minister of Dursley, Gloucestershire, the Revd Joseph Alleine at Bath, after his persecution under the Act of Uniformity, and Robert Frampton, when deprived of his office as Bishop of Gloucester, are known to have taught children on Sundays. Eighteenth-century founders of Sunday schools before 1780 form an impressive list, including John Wesley, the great preacher and founder of Methodism, Catherine Boevey, the beautiful, wealthy widow of Flaxley Abbey, Gloucestershire, the Revd Theophilus Lindsey of Catterick, Yorkshire, who inspired Mrs Cappe to follow his example at Bedale, Hannah Ball, a young lady Methodist of High Wycombe, Buckinghamshire, James Hey, the bobbin winder of Little Lever, near Bolton, the Revd David Simpson, Minister of Christ Church, Macclesfield, and the Revd Thomas Stock at Ashbury, Berkshire. Each has his or her own interesting story.

Several Sunday schools, of which Raikes had knowledge, had been set up in the city and county of Gloucester before he and the Revd Mr Stock established theirs. At least two of those who had already organized Sunday schools were alleged to have been instrumental in persuading Raikes to follow their example. Sophia Cooke, daughter of a Gloucester surgeon, is said to have kept a Sunday school in the city and she and Raikes had been first to conduct their Sunday scholars to church amid laughter and derisive remarks from bystanders. A more likely claimant to have influenced Raikes in his decision to set up Sunday schools might have been William King, a woollen card maker of Dursley, who in 1774 started gathering children together on Sundays in order to give them religious training and to teach them to read. King frequently visited Gloucester Castle Gaol to minister to those unfortunates under sentence of death, and it appears that he hoped, by means of his Sunday school, to prevent his scholars from ever breaking the law and risk suffering the disastrous consequences. Raikes, himself a frequent visitor to the gaol, knew and became friendly with King. During one of his visits to Gloucester, the Dursley businessman (his daughters later contended) called upon Raikes and as they walked together through the city convinced him of the need to establish Sunday schools for the youngsters they observed running wild through the streets.

Raikes stated that the idea originated for him when some business led him into the city suburbs where 'the lowest sort of people lived'. Seeing 'a group of children, wretchedly ragged at play in the streets' he had inquired of an inhabitant whether the children belonged to that district, whereupon the woman to whom he was speaking, appreciating his concern, described the behaviour of the children of the area on Sundays, when the factory was closed – 'the noise and riot . . . cursing and swearing'. 'This conversation suggested to me,' wrote Raikes, 'that it would be at least a harmless attempt, if it were productive of no good, should some little plan be formed to check this deplorable profanation of the Sabbath.'

If the founding of his Sunday school was 'owing to (the) accident', as Raikes described this chance conversation, and to the hope of peace and quiet on Sundays, reasons of much deeper significance soon became apparent to him. Before any of his contemporaries, he expressed the belief that 'A reformation in society seemed [to him] only practicable by establishing notices of duty, and practical habits of order and decorum, at an early stage.' Underlying the 'reformation' he envisaged, were the solutions to religious, moral, social, and economic problems of the day.

Raikes's first-hand knowledge of the suffering of those being punished under the cruel laws of eighteenth-century England undoubtedly provided motivation for the establishment and support of Sunday schools. He not only undertook philanthropic work among those confined in Gloucester Gaol and strove for prison reform, seeing as he did that prison life corrupted rather than corrected its inmates, but he reported in his newspaper the conditions in the gaol.

> The prisoners are locked up at night in a large apartment called the Main, with a chain run through each man's link; during the night they steal from each other, shoes, buckles, bread, or anything which it is possible to conceal . . . As there is no separation of the sexes in the day time, one of the women sentenced to long confinement is now ready to lie in, and would be destitute of every necessary for such a situation, had not a private beneficence placed a fund, for the relief of occasional distress, in the hands of one individual. In short, the inhabitants of this prison give a more affecting picture of the miseries entailed on mankind by the corruption of human nature, than it is in the power of imagination to paint.

Raikes also described the degradation to which convicts were reduced. In his editorial of 6 March 1786, he wrote:

On Wednesday last the keeper of the Castle set off for London with 14 convicts sentenced to transportation, chained together. Before the carriage drove off, one of them, named Isaac Rogers, a native of Cromhall, seeing a crowd of boys collected around, bade them to remember the shocking sight – so many of their fellow creatures, chained like dogs, going to be sold for slaves, because they had despised honest labour and its comfort in their own country. Several others added, 'What he has told you is very true, therefore take warning.'

The vivid portrayal in the columns of the *Gloucester Journal* of the public executions of prisoners convicted of capital offences such as housebreaking and horse stealing, show that in all probability Raikes himself witnessed the agonies and death throes of the condemned. Yet, as Raikes informed his readers, the sickening spectacle of hangings proved a poor deterrent to crime, and many of the offenders were often little more than youths. Raikes's report in the *Gloucester Journal* of 8 August 1785 of the execution of one James Hawkins for housebreaking showed clearly the need for children to attend Sunday schools.

Hawkins exhibited a melancholy proof of the truth of that expression, 'having the conscience seared with a hot iron' for tho' little more than 21 years of age, he was a shocking instance of the villainy which pervades the human heart, when the mind is destitute of every principle, and ignorance and vice are free from impose. He had never offered up a prayer to his Creator. He said he knew not how to pray. He was totally devoid of all sense of a future state.

Raikes believed that the incidence of crime could be reduced by instructing the neglected children of the poor on Sundays and he hoped that educated people, especially the clergy, within local communities would establish and supervise Sunday schools and those who could afford it would provide financial support. The printer had the vision to see the possibilities, and became the leading publicist of the Sunday-school movement. He regularly, but judiciously, reported the establishment and progress of Sunday schools in his newspapers. Correspondents provided plenty of evidence of Sunday schools being set up in Gloucestershire and the neighbouring counties. The account of 7 January 1788 from Cheltenham was typical.

Thro' the liberality of some distinguished characters, who visited our salutary spring last summer, seconded by the benevolent spirit of the inhabitants, four Sunday Schools were established here in the latter end of October, and about 100 of the most neglected children of the poor admitted. The behaviour of the children gaining upon the worthy persons who undertook the important care of inspection, it was determined that a reform in manners should be attended with comforts they had never before enjoyed; and yesterday it was agreed to make a little festival. Being assembled at the schools, the children walked in order to the church, where a numerous congregation was present to hear a discourse from the Rev. Mr Delabare, admirably calculated to inspire zeal for this species of charity. The text was taken from the 2nd verse of the 8th Psalm. 'Out of the mouths of babes and sucklings hast thou ordained strength.'

After divine service, the children, attended by their benefactors, went to the room appointed for their reception, where they shewed such specimens of their attainments, as might be expected from the great attention that had been paid them. Numbers had made considerable advancement in reading, and had, in some degree, altered the coarse manners and dialect incident to that state of neglect, from which they had been rescued, to the orderly behaviour and conversation attendant on better cultivation. But what is of higher import, by the hymns and prayers that were repeated, it might be hoped they were in the path of exchanging the licentious language of regardless profanation, for the power of prayer and thanksgiving to HIM, who alone is able to confirm and strengthen the efforts of humanity. The examination ended; a plentiful dinner was served up; and it was a scene for an epicure in philanthropy to behold many respectable people of both sexes officiating in the true spirit of primitive Christianity, in the service of these poor objects of their benevolence.

The close of the preacher's sermon gave so much satisfaction, said the writer, that he endeavoured to remember it.

The true objects of compassion are young persons left uninstructed, unrestrained, to the dangers of a corrupted world. Such, without the timely interposition of your christian spirit, would these have been, whose appearance now, not only gives your eye the pleasure of a beautiful and affecting spectacle, but your hearts the joy of beholding at once so many young candidates for the usefulness in this world, and endless felicity in the next. Amongst the poor our religion first had its rise; and we are following the original plan of providence, in making provision to reveal those things to babes, which the wise and prudent, in their own eyes, have hid from themselves.

Raikes himself obtained from other newspapers statistical information which showed the Sunday schools to be a national phenomenon. Insertions in the *Gloucester Journal* must have proved stimulating and encouraging to those who considered following his example. Raikes not only publicized the founding of Sunday schools and their anniversaries, he made available information about the organization, management, and conduct of Sunday schools, together with the results which could be achieved in the education of the children. He also publicized charity sermons preached for the benefit of Sunday schools and printed copies of these sermons to be sold for the same cause. His own conviction of the efficacy of the Sunday school as an agency for producing a 'reformation in society' is clearly reflected in his publicity campaign.

More effective, perhaps, in giving publicity to Sunday schools was the image of Raikes himself. Although he never mentioned his own name in his newpaper in connection with Sunday schools, the letters he wrote in answer to inquiries, and the eulogies written about him, made his name a symbol for the movement.

Richard Townley, a squire and magistrate of Belfield, near Rochdale, after reading a reprint of the paragraph inserted in the *Gloucester Journal* on 3 November 1783, wrote to the Mayor of Gloucester for information about Sunday schools. The mayor passed Townley's inquiry to Raikes who replied on 25 November 1783. This letter so impressed Townley that he wrote direct to Raikes for permission to have it published 'in such journals and newspapers as [he should] judge proper'. Having obtained Raikes's consent, Townley dispatched Raikes's letter to at least two northern newspapers: it appeared in its entirety in both the *Manchester Mercury* and the *Leeds Intelligencer* the next month, and in the following June it was published in the widely read *Gentleman's Magazine*. Other letters on the subject of Sunday schools written by Raikes to individuals were also sent to the press.

Raikes's influence on one of his correspondents had significant consequences in the establishment of Sunday schools. William Fox, a London businessman, a native of Clapton, Gloucestershire, having had his attention drawn to Raikes's letter in the papers and wishing to devote some of his wealth to those in need, wrote to Raikes. He explained that he was a member of the society being formed to carry 'into general use' a plan for establishing Sunday schools on similar lines to those of Raikes and requested Raikes to send him details so that he might win support for the idea when members met to discuss it. Raikes replied immediately answering specific questions raised by Fox on the worthwhileness of Sunday instruction and whether it was possible during the one day each week to teach children to read, but pointed out that he had written only the week before a letter on the subject of Sunday schools to Jonas Hanway (the well-known philanthropist) and suggested that Fox ask him 'for sight of it'.

Raikes's reply proved so encouraging that Fox approached Raikes's brothers, William and Thomas, inviting Thomas, who was a bank director, to chair the meeting of the society. When Thomas, for business reasons, declined, William Raikes took Fox to see Henry Thornton, the banker, but he too was unable to take the chair. Hanway was approached and accepted. However, the Sunday School Society was actually founded at a second meeting on 7 September 1785, with Henry Thornton as Chairman. Thornton became its first President and Thomas Raikes served on the committee. Fox and Raikes continued their correspondence and Raikes, perhaps at Fox's request, sent to the members of the Sunday School Society a full description of the progress of the Sunday schools at Painswick, Gloucestershire, which was later published in several magazines. Of the 330 children 'bred up in total ignorance' who attended Painswick Sunday School, '230 [could] read in the Bible of Testament, 80 [could] read the Sunday Scholar's Companion, and about 21 [were] in the alphabet,' stated Raikes.

It was a sight interesting and truly affecting. Young people lately more neglected than cattle in the field, ignorant, profane, filthy, clamorous, impatient of every restraint, were here seen cleanly, quiet, observant of order, submissive, courteous in behaviour and in conversation free from that vileness which marks our wretched vulgar.

Not surprisingly it was resolved unanimously at the general meeting of the Sunday School Society on 11 July 1787, 'that in consideration of the zeal and merits of Robert Raikes, Esq., of Gloucester, who may be considered as the original founder, as well as the liberal promoter, of Sunday Schools, he be admitted an honorary member of this society.' Raikes himself reported in his own newspaper the following August the extent of the Sunday School Society's activities and the development of the Sunday-school movement across the country.

At the last meeting of the Sunday School Society it was reported by the Committee that since the institution of the Society, they had established and assisted 432 schools, containing 27,949 scholars. In various parishes of the kingdom, the number of poor children now attended to on Sundays, amounts to it is said little less than 300,000.

The full story of Raikes's personal publicity campaign on behalf of the Sunday-school movement cannot be told here, but undoubtedly its height was reached when he was summoned to audience with George III and his Queen, Charlotte, at Windsor. Accounts of this reached the press, but then Raikes did not cringe in the limelight. He appears to have enjoyed it.

The eulogies written about Raikes, against which he made no protest, probably inspired many well-to-do to follow his example in founding and supporting Sunday schools. Were it possible here to discuss other aspects of his life – Raikes the family man, the businessman, the newspaper editor, the prison visitor, and the Sunday-school founder and teacher – comparisons might be made with the paragonic figure often depicted, and interesting conclusions drawn. Anne Yearsley, the Bristol milkwoman, for instance, referred to Raikes in 1785, in her poem 'On Promoting Sunday Schools' as a generous man

> Whose heart can mourn, whose manly eye can melt
> At the dread thought of human soul destroyed

having almost certainly never met Raikes and with no knowledge of his toughness. Her work was sponsored by Hannah More, and received over a thousand subscribers, many of elevated rank.

The epithet 'founder' of the Sunday-school movement is neither inaccurate nor misapplied, only limiting. That the Sunday-school movement began immediately after Raikes commenced his publicity campaign is unquestionable. Before 1783 Sunday schools were so few that writers referred to them by the names of their founders and teachers. After 3 November 1783, and Raikes's notable passage in the *Gloucester Journal* the increase of Sunday schools was phenomenal. But Raikes's contribution to his own generation and those immediately following was deeper rooted, farther reaching and more radical than is generally appreciated. The statement by John Richard Green in his work *A Short History of the English People* (1874) showed surprising accuracy: 'The Sunday schools established by Mr Raikes of Gloucester at the close of the century were the beginnings of popular education.'[1]

NOTE

1 For a fuller account see Frank Booth, *Robert Raikes of Gloucester*, National Christian Education Council, March 1980.

Raikes and Reform

Shirley Elliott

'As sure as God is in Gloucestershire' is an ancient saying. Its lush farmland attracted the establishment of several abbeys. It had strong links with several well-known martyrs, notably Bishop Hooper and William Tyndale, and by the eighteenth century it was the scene of intense activity in the religious revival of England.

A Gloucester man called George Whitefield was one of the most vigorous preachers of that century and was amongst the first to revive the principal truths which had produced the Protestant Reformation. He believed not only in preaching the gospel of Christ far and wide, but in living it, and rescued many from vice and ignorance. While he was studying at Oxford he visited and read to the prisoners in the gaol and met John and Charles Wesley and their 'Holy Club' friends. He preached his first sermon at St Mary de Crypt in Gloucester at about the same time that Robert Raikes was christened there.

When Whitefield preached, the congregation overflowed into the churchyards and consequently he did much of his preaching in the fields and market places. One spring day in 1739 he invited his old friend John Wesley to share in open-air preaching in Bristol. John, who had recently experienced a strong personal conversion, accepted, and 'proclaimed in the highways the glad tidings of salvation' to three thousand people. For the next half-century John Wesley travelled nearly a quarter of a million miles on horseback, Bible in hand, preparing his sermons as he rode along. His words moved the people and when they were expressed in poetry and music they absorbed the gospel message more quickly and took it home with them that way – many of them could not read. (Hymn singing was not allowed in Anglican churches.) John Wesley wisely used his power of stirring the emotions of his listeners and his message brought them a deep personal religion.

Both John Wesley and George Whitefield were known to the Raikes family. Wesley visited the Raikes when he was in Gloucester and Robert Raikes was amongst the crowd of several thousand that heard Wesley preach at five in the morning. Whitefield had contributed to the *Gloucester Journal* in the time of Raikes senior, condemning conditions in the city gaol.

Raikes senior was a philanthropist. A confident Yorkshireman, he was in trouble with the House of Commons for publishing a report of certain parliamentary procedures in his paper, but he wasn't a man to give in easily if he thought he was right. He was against the waste of grain for the distillation of spirits, the inhuman treatment of criminals (especially debtors) and the barbarous practice of cock-fighting. Raikes died in 1757 leaving his eldest son Robert to bring up his younger brothers and sisters and take control of his printing business and the *Gloucester Journal*.

Robert Raikes was the only printer between Exeter and Hereford, in the whole of Wales and part of the Midlands. Consequently he was a person of influence although in those days the press was objective, not subjective. 'The editor of a weekly paper', wrote Raikes, 'is under a necessity of suppressing pieces that might be an ornament to it, that matters of opinion may not take the place of matters of fact.' Raikes used his paper to expose the conditions in which the poor lived in Gloucester and to advertise the patent medicines he sold for cancer, V.D., and scurvy. He was a trustee of the Northgate Turnpike which was responsible for the London road out of Gloucester as far as Crickley Hill and Birdlip – the better the roads the faster the Flying Coach could travel with his news from London.

Gloucester at this time was moving into what we now term the Industrial Revolution. The city was the home of the pin industry – complementary to the county's main occupation of weaving. Adam Smith, writing in 1775, quoted the pin-making industry as a successful example of the division of labour. One man working on his own 'could not make twenty' pins a day, whereas the group of men working in such a way that 'one man draws out the wire, another straights it, a third cuts it, a fourth points it, a fifth grinds it at the top for receiving the head' and so on would increase individual output to 'four thousand eight hundred pins a day'. Many pinners – men, women, and children – worked at home and were having to compete with the beginnings of mass production. They all worked very long hours but unemployment was becoming a serious problem. The population was increasing considerably and in 1760 the first of the Enclosure Acts had driven country men into the towns. Skilled men could wander from town to town looking for work and, finding none, could become vagrants. There was no state relief for the unemployed – the Church was the nation's almoner.

Debt was something to be feared because debtors were thrown into Gloucester's filthy overcrowded gaol. The debtor's room was nineteen feet long and eleven feet wide. A hole had been knocked in the wall for light and air. The day room for all the other prisoners was 11' 9" × 10' 7". The walls were not whitewashed and men and women prisoners were not separated. Many prisoners died from smallpox and gaol fever and children were born there. Yet when Raikes took Howard (the prison reformer) round the prison in 1773, he considered it one of the better gaols. Robert Raikes and a few religious men were the only visitors and Raikes regularly gave the debtors a few pence to buy bread – the prison authorities made no allowance for the support of minor offenders.

'From private benefactions placed in his hand last winter . . . the Printer has been enabled to give an allowance of twopenny-worth of bread per day to debtors, who, not able to pay for a bed, are obliged to lie upon straw and without such assistance must have perished for want.' Through the medium of his paper, Raikes was able to act as link between the prisoners and those who would help. Another day he wrote, 'The High Sheriff took indefatigable pain . . . at the risk of his own life to render the gaol free from contagion.' The distemper had gone – only sores remained. Raikes appealed for a 'benevolent person who could send me some old linen . . . it would contribute greatly to their recovery.' A year later, in 1785, he wrote:

> Our gaol at this time exhibits a melancholy scene of wretchedness and profligacy beyond the example of any former period . . . the naked are given shirts which are promptly stolen by other prisoners. In the daytime the sexes are not separated . . . increasing depravity. At night in the main, a chain running through each man's link . . . they steal from each other anything possible to conceal.

And later, Raikes was reporting a worse situation. 'No less than eleven criminals were brought in since Sunday, most of them for capital offences, housebreaking, highway robbery and sheepstealing . . . there are now one hundred and twenty-five prisoners. The number at the period of the year was formerly about eighty.'

37

During that same year 'a freeholder', recognizing that unemployment was one of the causes of social disorder, wrote to the printer 'especially for the attention of prison reformers', suggesting the establishment of 'suitable houses of industry' a few miles apart which would occupy the unemployed, keep them out of mischief, and lower the poor rate. But nobody seemed to be doing anything and a year later a frustrated Raikes wrote: 'If government or the magistrates of the country seek not for some expedient of removing the plea of want of work, the excess of wickedness among the common people will destroy all the comforts to be enjoyed from civil society.'

The problem of unemployment could not be solved so easily, but it is interesting to note that there were people concerned in remedying the cause of starvation and debt rather than as hitherto being content with punishing the offender, then feeding him with the churchman's charity.

The high price of corn and consequently of bread had moved fifty-three prominent citizens of Gloucester, including Raikes, to send the following petition in January 1766 to the county's two M.P.s.

We the Aldermen, Sheriffs, Common Council and Principal Inhabitants of the city of Gloucester . . . influenced by the ties of humanity, cannot help commiserating the present distressed state of the poor, on account of the scarcity and exorbitant price of the most essential necessities of life . . . We esteem it our duty to apply to you . . . for an immediate prohibition of the Exportation of corn . . . for removing this national grievance . . . to increase the welfare and interests of the whole community.

Raikes quoted the price of corn in his paper every week and so was aware of its high price. What also angered him was the misuse of corn for making intoxicating liquor and he advocated temperance in his *Journal*. Alcohol as much as unemployment was a cause of the high population of Gloucester gaol.

The people sent in are neither disappointed soldiers nor sailors, but chiefly frequenters of ale-house and skittle-alleys . . . The ships about to sail for Botany Bay will carry about one thousand miserable creatures, who might have lived perhaps happily in this country had they been early taught good principles and to avoid the danger of associating with those who make sobriety and industry objects of their ridicule.

The long journey on a crowded ship was probably worse than the actual exile. Raikes's interest in the prisoners went with them as far as these transport ships through his correspondents. Transportation was preferable to execution – executions for stealing were plentiful and together with cock-fighting and bull-baiting provided entertainment for the unruly crowds.

Acts of vandalism in the nearby Forest of Dean prompted Raikes to warn people of the severe penalties which certain crimes could incur. For stealing forest timber: seven years transportation; breaking hedges of forest enclosure: public whipping by the hangman at the end of every month; setting forest fences on fire: death.

Reading through the *Gloucester Journal* of two hundred years ago it is evident that Raikes the printer was greatly concerned with law and order. His paper had a wide circulation covering a few hundred square miles. But everyone could not read, especially among the lower classes (it was a very class conscious society), so obviously his warnings about law-breaking were not heard by all who would have benefited from his advice, though sometimes the few who could read would read to groups of their illiterate friends. Raikes had encouraged prisoners to read to each other and to teach each other. His interest in promoting literacy might tempt the cynic to suggest that an increase in the circulation of his newspaper was his real motive. Such a criticism would be extremely ill-informed and unfair, for once the prisoners could read there was plenty of other material to attract their interest.

Jean-Jacques Rousseau the French philosopher was writing a number of influential works which provoked the Church authorities and were to inspire the revolutionaries in France. 'Men are born free', Rousseau wrote, 'and everywhere they are in chains'.

Across the Atlantic Thomas Paine published a pamphlet called *Common Sense*. Born into a poor Norfolk family he ridiculed the British constitutional system and the monarchy and was successful in influencing public opinion in favour of independence. He wrote:

England since the conquest, hath known some few good monarchs, but groaned beneath a much larger number of bad ones; yet no man in his senses can say that their claim under William the Conqueror is a very honourable one. A French bastard landing with an armed bandetti, and establishing himself King of England against the consent of the natives, is in plain terms a very paltry rascally original.

Also in America, the Virginia Bill of Rights was published. It declared that 'when any government shall be found inadequate . . . a majority of the community hath an indubitable, unalienable and indefeasable right to reform, alter or abolish it . . .' and later that 'excessive bail ought not to be required, nor excessive fines imposed, nor cruel and unusual punishments inflicted'. Thomas Jefferson, in reforming the Penal Code reduced the number of crimes punishable by death to murder by duelling, murder, and treason.

These revolutionary rumblings would not have escaped the attention of Raikes who regularly received the *London Gazette* and no doubt read some of the tracts being circulated. His friends warned him of the dangers of teaching the masses to read, but he would not change his mind. He also remained a stern disciplinarian and applauded the strictness of the magistrates. 'The thanks of the public are highly due to the magistrates who enforce laws made for the maintenance of decency and good morals. Behaviour disgraceful to civil society is not suffered here to escape with impunity.' Ten years after the publication of the Virginia Bill of Rights, Raikes was reporting almost casually the execution of men for stealing and highway robbery and the transportation of women to Africa for receiving stolen goods. Raikes wanted to change conditions but not the system.

Could this be because he was intent on self-preservation? He was an affluent and influential man and he could have felt the need for the support of the lower classes in the event of rebellion. But Raikes and his father before him had shown their concern for the prisoners of Gloucester gaol long before revolution was in the air and the walk through the narrow, muddy, garbage-strewn streets of Gloucester and the risk of smallpox or typhoid in the germ-ridden gaol, were a more immediate and greater hazard to himself and his family than anything that might happen in the political world. It took many years of prison visiting for him to realize that the best way of im-proving prison conditions was to prevent people being turned into prisoners. Childhood is the time of character formation, so Raikes turned his attention to children.

In a letter to the *Gentleman's Magazine* in 1783, Raikes recalled the incident which began this part of his philanthropic work:

Some business having taken one into the suburbs of the city where the lowest of the people (who are principally employed in the pin manufactury) chiefly reside, I was struck with concern at seeing a group of children, wretchedly ragged, at play in the street. I asked an inhabitant whether these children belonged to that part of the town, and lamented their misery and idleness. 'Ah sir' said the woman, 'could you take a view of this part of the town on a Sunday, you would be shocked indeed; for then the street is filled with multitudes of the wretches, who, released on that day from employment, spend their time in noise and riot, playing at chuck, cursing and swearing in a manner so horrid as to convey to any serious mind an idea of hell . . . their parents, totally abandoned themselves have no idea of instilling into the minds of their children, principles to which they themselves are entire strangers.'

Raikes obtained from his informant the names of four 'decent well disposed' women and hired them to teach children on a Sunday. The teachers were to instruct the children in small classes 'in reading and church catechism'. The year was 1780. Several other people had started Sunday schools during the previous decade in nearby villages and towns like Nailsworth, Painswick, Dursley, and Paganhill, but they failed to have the impact that Raikes's schools achieved. It could have been because they were Dissenters' schools.

Raikes was part of the establishment, an Anglican and wealthy. He went to a service at the Cathedral on Sunday mornings and after that his business as printer and editor kept him busy until late at night because the *Journal* was printed on Mondays. During the week he regularly attended the seven o'clock morning service at the Cathedral. This was probably as much for business reasons as for worship, but Raikes wrote of some Sunday School children,

these little ragamuffins have taken it into their heads to frequent the early morning prayers . . . held at Cathedral at 7 o'clock . . . near fifty this morning . . . they assemble at the house of one of their mistresses and walk before her to church, two and two . . . after service they all come round to me to make their bow . . . the great principle I inculcate is, to be kind and good natured to each other;

not to provoke one another; to be dutiful to parents; not to offend God by cursing and swearing, and such little plain precepts as all may comprehend . . . the Society for Promoting Christian Knowledge sometimes makes me a present of a parcel of Bibles, Testaments, etc. which I distribute as rewards for the deserving.

Raikes enjoyed 'botanizing in human nature' and going among the children

doing them little kindnesses, distributing trifling rewards, and ingratiating myself with them . . . I am told they are much afraid of my displeasure. If the glory of God be promoted in any, even the smallest degree, society must reap some benefit. If good seed be sown in the mind at an early period of human life, though it shows itself not again for many years, it may please God, at some future period to cause it to spring up and to bring forth a plentiful harvest.

Sunday school children were given the short-term benefit of a full stomach and long-term improvement in education and moral living. At Mitcheldean Sunday School the children were given a three-penny loaf each by an anonymous donor. 'Such little encouragements have great effect in exciting among the children an emulation to deserve the notice of their superiors, by a quiet and orderly behaviour.' Many of the Gloucester children were clothed in rags and were referred to as Raikes's 'ragged regiment', but money was raised for them to have decent clothes and these, because they were uniform, distinguished them as 'Raikes children'.

In 1786 Raikes wrote of Painswick Sunday School, 'To relieve the parish of the burden of clothing these poor creatures, such children bring a penny each Sunday . . . have that penny doubled . . . admirable effect.' These hardworking children were being taught to manage their money and not to waste time, for they had 'their books by their looms to read when the thread breaks'. It didn't occur to Raikes to publicize the exploitation of child labour.

The Sunday-school system grew rapidly and effectively and John Wesley was delighted to see Sunday schools springing up wherever he went. Three years after their establishment, Raikes felt able to make the first announcement in the *Gloucester Journal* on the success of the Sunday-school system, but without mentioning his own name. He wrote of the children 'they begin to give proofs that those persons are mistaken who consider the lower orders of mankind as incapable of improvement'.

In 1786 he was writing of a church service in Painswick:

> young people lately more neglected than cattle in the field, ignorant, profane, filthy, clamourous, impatient of any restraint were here seen clearly, quiet, observant of order, submissive, courteous in behaviour and in conversation, free from that vileness which marks our wretched vulgar . . . the collection of £24 or £25 might be deemed a good one. My astonishment was great . . . £57. This may be accounted for from the security which the establishment of Sunday Schools has given to the property of every individual in the neighbourhood . . . farmers can now leave their house and garden etc. and frequent public worship without danger of depredation.

It is hard to believe that the change in behaviour was as great as Raikes claimed, especially as there were more prisoners than ever in Gloucester gaol, but the population was increasing and Raikes's influence was mainly limited to children and their parents. However, Sunday schools were attracting a lot of attention. When Raikes was in Windsor he was invited to an audience with Queen Charlotte, who said that 'she envied those who had the power of doing good by thus personally promoting the welfare of society in giving instruction and morality to the general mass of the common people, a pleasure from which by her position she was debarred'. Her husband, George III, visited a Sunday school in Brentford and wished that 'every child in my kingdom should be taught to read the Bible'.

Before long, many thousands of children were attending Sunday schools. Raikes's 'grain of mustard seed' had grown, and in 1794 he published a *Sunday Scholar's Companion* which contained graded scriptural sentences for the child to read as his proficiency improved. The foreword would be offensive nowadays.

> The idea of Sunday Schools, for introducing some degree of Civilization among the children of the vulgar . . . A gentleman who stands one of the foremost as an advocate for this simple but practicable scheme of raising the common people from that brutal ignorance, and lamentable corruption of morals now so universally deplored is Revd Mr Moore . . . of Kent. . . .

That Raikes did so much for children of the lower classes and refrained from mentioning the misdemeanours of the rich, at first suggests that he was smugly satisfied with his own class. Mr Moore's sermon shows that there was a different reason.

> The profanation of Sunday . . . the high in station treat the day and all its services with a sovereign contempt: those of middling rank employ it either in settling their worldly accounts, or in forming such arrangements as constantly interfere with their regular attendance at church; while the common sort consume it in common pastimes and diversions, if not in drunkenness and debauchery.

The rich had education and opportunity to make good of their lives. Raikes was offering the poor something which the self-satisfied middle and upper classes had rejected. But was their lack of religion the fault of the well-to-do?

They mostly belonged to the Anglican Church which was at this time in the depths of spiritual sickness. Many of the clergy were from the aristocracy, had more than one living, and chose pleasant country parishes. Frequently they were absent from their parishes for long periods, so funerals took place some time after bodies were buried. When such clergy bought a living they often bought a book of sermons to last them their lifetime – they had neither the time nor the desire to develop spiritual thoughts for they were perpetually hunting and drinking. Wesley, a lifelong member of the Church of England, referred to their bishops as 'mitred infidels'. Little wonder that the members of these churches were as indifferent as Moore describes. In some places, rationalism was replacing the Christian gospel.

A reaction to orthodoxy and rationalism was the Evangelical revival. It emphasized the personal religious experience of sin and of salvation through faith and had been greatly influenced by the Pietists and Moravian Church in Germany who met in small prayer groups that encouraged Bible study and daily living according to the spirit of Christ. John and Charles Wesley and George Whitefield had been greatly influenced by the Moravians and they led the Evangelical revival in Britain. Some of the higher classes in society were moved to do good works. Some were Anglican but there was a strong Quaker influence. Elizabeth Fry and John Howard are well known for their prison reforms. Sarah Trimmer and Hannah More emulated Robert Raikes's Sunday school work. Raikes's distant cousin, William Wilberforce, was a great influence in the abolition of slavery. John Newton and William Cowper wrote hymns which are well known to us today.

These people were moved to apply the principles they had absorbed from Scripture to the needs they saw around them. Wilberforce was the only one to strive for reform through the political system because that was the only way the world-wide system of slavery could be effectively attacked. Nevertheless he remained as politically unencumbered as possible by standing for parliament as an independent.

Raikes saw his own role simply. 'It is that part of our Saviour's character which I aim at imitating: "He went about doing good".' So as Christ made no attempt at social reform by overthrowing the Roman rulers and their Jewish parasites, but threw all his efforts into reforming people, so Raikes concentrated on reforming as many people as possible by giving them a knowledge of God and consequently Christian standards and aspirations. Raikes was not trying to soft soap the poorer people into accepting oppression in this life with the promise of glory in the next. As we have seen in his prison and Sunday-school work, he personally equated riches with responsibility.

A friend of Raikes, the Revd William Lewelyn, had written to him on the subject of the love of God. In his reply Raikes wrote, 'Were all men by such communication to provoke each other to good works manifesting their love to the giver of all good by imitating his beneficence in their conduct to their fellow creatures, what a happy world we should live in. . . .'

Chastising those who looked for excuses to do nothing, he wrote in the *Gentleman's Magazine*:

> The minds of men have taken hold on that prejudice that we are to do nothing on the Sabbath Day which may be deemed labour, and therefore we are to be excused from all application of mind as well as body. The rooting out of this prejudice is the point I aim at as my favourite object.

(This was a principle very convenient to him as he worked his compositors hard on Sundays.)

> Our Saviour takes particular pains to manifest that whatever tended to promote the health and happiness of our fellow

creatures, were sacrifices particularly acceptable on that day . . .
Let our patriots employ themselves in rescuing their fellow
countrymen from that despotism which tyrannical passions and
vicious inclinations exercise over them; and they will find that
true liberty and national welfare are more efficiently promoted
than by any reform in parliament.

(The middle classes were clamouring for the franchise.)

Raikes saw local needs and challenged those who ignored them.
Reporting on a sermon given in Oxford on 'The duty of preaching
the gospel to Mahometan and Gentoo subjects in India', he wrote,
'Charity begins at home' and tells of a Forest of Dean clergyman
who had informed him that many dying people he had visited had
never heard of Jesus Christ and never been taught to 'offer up
prayer to the Deity'. The plight of people touched Raikes. Underneath his hard-headed business exterior he was a tender-hearted,
even emotional man.

This sensitivity is reflected in his love of the Psalms. Raikes wrote
in a letter: 'I am never in so proper a frame as whilst I am reading
or repeating passages from that heavenly composition. They are my
chief comfort and consolation when any distress approaches. They
furnish the language of thanksgiving when the heart rejoices. . . .' It
is said that Isaiah 53 which foretells the suffering and sacrifice of
Jesus, also made a deep impression on him. The older children in
his Sunday School learnt some of the hymns of Isaac Watts
(1674–1748). Some of these were based on Psalms but all expressed
the Evangelical spirit, one of the best known being,

> When I survey the wondrous cross
> On which the Prince of Glory died
> My richest gain I count but loss
> And pour contempt on all my pride.
>
> Were the whole realm of nature mine
> That were an offering far too small!
> Love so amazing, so divine,
> Demands my soul, my life, my all.

The same spirit prompted Raikes to write in 1793:

I see my own unworthiness more clearly, and with this plea I go
more boldly to the throne of Grace . . . having faith and confi-

dence in his power to restore. Without this hope of relief, the pressure of my sins would be a burden too heavy for me to bear.

However this is language which I speak only to you and to my own heart. The world would laugh. They conceive that notorious crimes are all that we have to guard against. But you and I have not so learned Christ!

It is hard to imagine this critical self-examination going on inside the mind of this portly gentleman that various people described as wearing 'cocked hat, a bob wig, an eyeglass, a claret coloured coat with silver buttons, tight fitting nankeen breeches and white stockings', having a 'swaggering walk'. He alone knew what was underneath. We have seen traces of his self-esteem in his communications about the Sunday school. We know he was a stern disciplinarian, but a streak of something akin to cruelty appeared in the *Journal* one day:

Whereas John Jones, Apprentice to R. Raikes has left his master's service: Notice is hereby given that if any person shall harbour or employ such runaway Apprentice, they shall be prosecuted with all the vigour of the law. As he has been detected in the vilest falsehoods and acts of dishonesty, the public are cautioned to beware of him.

John Jones had done something very wrong, we do not know what exactly, but need the whole affair have been broadcast in the *Journal*? It is the only announcement of that nature. Not only was the lad ruined but there could have been unfortunate consequences for his family. At least Raikes was conscious of his own shortcomings and asked a friend to pray for him, 'the vilest, frailest, weakest of your fellow creatures'.

What the citizens of eighteenth-century Gloucester thought was pride in this 'bustling, pompous city magnate' was just as much patronage. Evangelicalism was concerned with reforming the character of the individual to Christ-like standards, not with reforming the class system; hence Raikes could write to the Revd William Lewelyn: 'It is looking up to Jesus . . . through the medium of humility and a due sense of our own vileness and unworthiness, that appears to me the only means of following him whither he has gone before' and yet include the following prayer in his *Sunday Scholar's Companion*: 'Grant that as we increase in years, so we may increase in all goodness and piety. Make us thankful for these Opportunities of Instruction that are given us by the charity of our benefactors . . . to be grateful and obedient to our superiors for all their favours.' How obnoxious to twentieth-century ears!

But if Raikes expected those beneath him to know their place, he suffered the same fate from the opposite end of the social strata! Miss Burney, Queen Charlotte's Lady in Waiting, had been conducted round Gloucester's new prison by Raikes. Recording her visit to his house she described him and his family.

> Mr Raikes is not a man that, without a previous disposition toward approbation, I should have greatly admired. He is somewhat too flourishing, somewhat too forward, somewhat too voluble; but he is worthy, benevolent, good natured and good hearted, and therefore the overflowing of successful spirits and delighted vanity must meet with some allowance. His wife is a quiet unpretending woman; his daughters common sort of country misses. They seem to live with great hospitality, plenty and good cheer. . . .

Anybody of consequence visiting Gloucester visited Raikes. He escorted them all to the nearest Sunday school in Grey Friars – Sunday schools and philanthropy had become fashionable. But in forming a fair critical opinion of Raikes, one has to look at him in historical perspective and in the spirit of the age in which he lived. His was not an egalitarian society. Could he have done more in the field of education, the abolition of child labour or prison reform? Man learnt to build houses before he built skyscrapers. Raikes and some of his contemporaries laid the foundations of society as we know it and we have benefited from the good things they did and learned from the mistakes they made. Considering the limits of their vision, their work was considerable. The Church should have been active in tending its flock instead of leaving it to the local printer to light the torch of the Sunday-school movement and the subsequent education system.

Fortunately it was a work for which he was uniquely suited. There was the family tradition of philanthropy, he was wealthy, he had the responsibility of bringing up his younger brothers and sisters when he himself was relatively young, and he specialized in spreading information. He was a man with a mission which he pursued with abundant energy to the end of his days. He 'tried' where many others looked the other way. As an old man he recalled to the Quaker

Joseph Lancaster the moment when he decided to help under-
privileged children.

'Pause here', said the old man. Then uncovering his head and
closing his eyes, he stood for a moment in silent prayer. Then
turning towards his friend, while the tears rolled down his cheeks,
he said: 'This is the spot on which I stood when I saw the
destitution of the children and the desecration of the Sabbath by
the inhabitants of the city. As I asked, "Can nothing be done?"
a voice answered, "Try". I did try, and see what God has
wrought.'

Part II

*Nineteenth-Century
Developments*

Urban Growth and the Social Role of the Stockport Sunday School
c. 1784–1833

Malcolm Dick

I

Accelerating urban expansion in the late eighteenth and early nineteenth centuries presented the British with unprecedented problems. Several observers of the new industrial towns perceived the apparent results of this growth with alarm. Religious observance withered, traditional ties of obligation and gratitude were cut, and the urban poor floated in a sea of iniquity to serve as prey for the sharks of radicalism and infidelity. The conservative and evangelical writers and philanthropists who feared social and spiritual collapse were determined to create an ordered and Christian environment.[1] One of the most important representatives of this school of thought was Thomas Chalmers, a Scottish economist and theologian. Chalmers was shocked by the depravity of the urban poor in Glasgow, and in several works, especially the influential *Christian and Civic Economy of Large Towns*, he offered his perceptions of the problem, and developed possible solutions to it.[2] One means of introducing genuine religious commitment and a respect for authority, he believed, was the Sunday school. He declared that the establishment of these institutions, integrated within the local community, supported by the upper and middle classes, and staffed by former scholars, would be an effective means of overcoming immorality.[3] Not only would they help to convert the masses, but they might 'reclaim the whole of our present generation, to a kindliness for the upper classes that is now unfelt . . . by the ministration of such a moral influence among the young, as would serve to exalt humble life'.[4]

Chalmers was writing in the early decades of the nineteenth century, but Sunday schools had started in the 1780s. In many towns, they already presented their evangelical and conservative message. One of the most important institutions was the Stockport Sunday School which had emerged in 1784 as an educational agency

53

in this cotton-manufacturing town. It developed in the nineteenth century to become the largest Sunday school in the world.[5] The School provided a means by which the industrialists and traders of Stockport could combat the supposed moral illiteracy of the poor. The Stockport Sunday School attempted to rescue children from the dangerous influence of their social and working environment and the threats posed by religious, political, and economic heresy. This paper attempts to analyse the ways in which its promoters and managers perceived this role, by focusing upon the following: first, the socio-economic context of the school's existence, secondly, the social location of its managers, and thirdly, the reactions of these individuals towards the supposed problems of the town: the poor, family life, the effects of the factory system, and working-class radicalism.

II

This part of the paper focuses upon the socio-economic context of the School's existence.[6] Such an examination is needed to understand the doctrines and perceptions of its promoters. It is always difficult to relate ideas and images to material conditions, but the promoters were deeply concerned with the kind of town Stockport was and what it could become. This section analyses the industrial development of the town, the different experiences of rich and poor, and the form taken by working-class radicalism in Stockport.

One of the earliest centres of the factory system, Stockport experienced a rapid growth in population as manufacturing expanded. A silk industry developed in the eighteenth century, but it was supplanted by cotton textiles. In 1795 there were twenty-three cotton factories, and in 1822 forty-seven existed in the town. The latter were worked by sixty-two steam engines and water wheels, and the largest mill was owned by Peter Marsland, one of the committee members of the Stockport Sunday School.[7] The urban environment was dominated by the factory.

> The town stretches along the south bank of the river in the form of a large amphitheatre; and the manufactories, rising in tiers above each other, when lighted with the brilliant gaseous vapours of modern discovery, presents in the evenings of the winter months a towering illumination of imposing grandeur, of which it is difficult to convey an adequate idea.[8]

As the number of factories grew, population increased as people moved to the town to obtain work. In the first thirty years of the nineteenth century, Stockport experienced an expansion of population from 14,830 in 1801 to 25,469 in 1831.[9]

Industrial growth increased the prosperity of manufacturing and trading interests. Many of the principal subscribers of the Sunday School belonged to this class, and a substantial number of these were able to afford annual donations of twenty to fifty pounds.[10] Peter Marsland, undoubtedly one of the wealthiest, owned a mansion in the adjacent country, 'standing alone in the midst of a beautiful garden, with its greenhouses and pleasant walks on the banks of the river Mersey, which flowed along as a clear and limpid stream'.[11] Luddites, experiencing the results of a trade depression, and protesting against the use of the power loom, showed little respect for his dwelling when they smashed its windows in 1812.[12]

In fact, for the lower classes, expanding industry did not guarantee prosperity. Although wages may have been higher than in labouring occupations in the countryside, an accumulation of trade depressions recurring with monotonous regularity between 1788 and 1830[13] caused sporadic unemployment and wage reductions. Poverty was widespread, especially when allied to the exorbitant price of provisions.[14] Not surprisingly poor rates were very high.[15] The experiences of members of the lower classes during these years of depression were collected from the memories of Stockport people themselves, by a local historian in the late nineteenth century:

> One says, 'Times were very bad and provisions very scarce and dear. . . . The bread generally eaten was nearly black and mixed with barley and rye. . . .'
> . . . . Another says, 'Those were bad times. My father was an operative spinner, a good workman, and very careful, but even with us, we could only get wheaten bread as a luxury. My parents bought a white loaf once a month, and it was divided amongst us with the greatest care, like sweetmeats among children. Tea, coffee, and sugar we never tasted, our food was oat-cake and oat-meal-porridge with milk and water, and only very occasionally a little treacle.'[16]

Undoubtedly the sufferings of poverty, allied to the alienating effect of factory labour and the erosion of traditional spinning and weaving skills through mechanization, increased discontent. The

Stockport Sunday School operated in a town at the centre of working-class radicalism and the members of the institution's committee focused upon this situation,[17] as a subsequent part of the paper reveals. When the Combination Act of 1799 made trade unions illegal, workers still petitioned for wage increases and strikes took place in 1808 when an unsuccessful attempt was made to form a General Union.[18] Stockport also featured in the Luddite disturbances in 1812. Fourteen Luddites were condemned to death in the town, although only two were in fact executed.[19] There was further discontent in 1815, partly caused by a collapse of the cotton trade, an influx of demobilized ex-servicemen competing for jobs after the end of the Napoleonic Wars, and an increase in the price of corn.[20] Manufacturers were sufficiently concerned by the last problem to protest to Parliament about the inflationary effect of the Corn Laws.[21] In 1816 an attempt by workers to combine was punished with sentences of hard labour by a local magistrate, the Revd C. Prescott, a promoter of Anglican Sunday schools in the town.[22] In 1817 the Blanketeers were supported in Stockport. Several meetings were held, and some were suppressed by the military and special constables.[23] In the same year, a radical Sunday school was formed in the town, an alternative educational institution to that of the Stockport Sunday School.[24] Further strikes broke out in 1818 amongst spinners and weavers. When one manufacturer imported blackleg labour to work for him, his mill was besieged by rioters who had to be dispersed by the Yeomanry.[25] In the same year the Stockport Political Union was formed to campaign for political reform.[26] 'Orator' Hunt spoke in the town at the beginning of 1819, and was escorted by a crowd of supporters to Manchester.[27] Several mass meetings, in fact, were held in the town during the year, to demand reforms, and on at least one occasion the request of the magistrates to disperse was disregarded.[28] A large number of Stockport people – one estimate gives five thousand men – met at St Peter's Fields in Manchester to hear Hunt speak on 16 August 1819.[29] This event, of course, culminated in the Peterloo Massacre. Radicalism appeared to be quiescent in the early 1820s, but in 1826 political meetings were held again and suppressed and in 1829 the Riot Act was read in the town.[30] The experiences of these years, added to similar incidents in the 1830s, led to considerable friction between masters and men.[31] This divided society provided the context within which the Stockport Sunday School operated.

III

This section concentrates upon the promoters and managers of the institution. An understanding of their background and assumptions is important for appreciating how they perceived the people whom they attempted to educate in their school. These men were Evangelical in religion, being influenced by the growth of Wesleyan Methodism in the town. In occupation they were almost all traders and manufacturers. The Stockport Sunday School began in association with the Hillgate Meeting House, which was the oldest Methodist chapel in Stockport.[32] Between 1784 and 1793 the school associated with this chapel was linked with other Sunday schools which were administered by an interdenominational committee of gentlemen.[33] The Hillgate Meeting House School was the most successful and largely through the influence of Joseph Mayer, himself to become the leading figure in the early history of the Stockport Sunday School, it separated from the parental committee in 1794 and grew rapidly.[34] In 1806 a custom-built institution was erected to accommodate increased numbers.[35] The spiritual message of the establishment was Wesleyan Methodist in emphasis. This Evangelical doctrine stressed the natural depravity of man and the need for repentance and religious commitment to overcome human sinfulness. Its adherents were likely to be very critical of those who failed to live up to its exacting standards. The social message of the doctrine was conservative, supporting the maintenance of the social order, obedience to established authority and the law, and the acceptance of social distinctions based upon wealth. Those who adhered to these beliefs were hostile to those who threatened to disturb or overthrow existing society.[36]

The promoters and managers of the School were overwhelmingly manufacturers and traders in the town. One student of the institution, Thomas W. Laqueur, has claimed that it was managed entirely by industrialists.[37] Although some of the leading figures such as Matthew and Joseph Mayer were factory owners, an analysis of the occupations of members of the committee using commercial directories does not bear out Laqueur's contention. Only a third of committee members for 1815–16 and 1821–22 can be described as industrialists (Table 1); it is more accurate to characterize the School as the creation of traders and factory owners.[38] It is reasonable to expect that these men might use the School to protect their interests,

TABLE I
Occupations of the Committee of the Stockport Sunday School
1815–16 and 1821–22

OCCUPATIONS	1815–16	1821–22
Cotton spinners and manufacturers	5	5 (6)[b]
Cotton manufacturers and linen and woollen drapers	1	1
Linen and woollen drapers	5	4 (5)[c]
Hosiers	1	1
Hat manufacturers/hatters	2	2
Nursery and seedsmen	1	1
Dealers in food[a]	3	4
Timber dealers	2	1
Solicitors		1
Esquires/gentlemen/sons of gentlemen		3 (2)[b]
Tobacconists		1
Insurance agents		1
Unknown	6	7 (6)[c]
TOTAL	26	32

[a] includes cheesemongers, corn and flour dealers, bakers and grocers.

[b] according to the 1816–17 directory, Peter Marsland Esq. is given no occupation for these years; however in the directory for 1821–22 he is described as a manufacturer.

[c] there is no reference to Samuel Dodge in the directory for 1821–22, but in the directory for 1816–17 he is described as a linen and woollen draper.

but it would be wrong to say that they used the institution as a means of capitalist social control, promoting the punctuality and work-discipline of the factory work-force. Although the School stressed the importance of virtues such as deference and hard work, it was strongly critical of some aspects of factory employment. In addition it also emphasized the importance of qualities such as a morally cohesive family life, which had little direct relationship with the mental attitudes required by factory operatives.

IV

According to the promoters of the Stockport Sunday School, the urban poor were lacking in religion and morality. The supposed depravity of the lower orders threatened economic prosperity and the religious and social order and, moreover, required the intervention of a new agency, the Sunday school, to create social cohesion and spiritual commitment in the town.

In 1795, the report of the Hillgate Meeting House School appealed to local tradesmen to support an enterprise which would prevent 'Vicious Habits', such as idleness, profligacy, and dishonesty, by 'instilling into the minds of Youth, the principles of Industry, Religion, and Justice.'[39] A report of 1796 asserted that, although the poor suffered from their poverty, the evils resulting from their depravity were greater than those arising from their economic situation.[40] In 1802 a report welcomed the return of peace between Britain and France, but regretted that it had not been accompanied by an improvement in the morality of the poor.[41] In fact:

> drunkenness and intemperance, idleness and disorder, revelry and wantonness are carried to their greatest excess. If these things do not provoke the incensed majesty of Heaven to inflict national or provincial judgements again upon us, they will certainly bring individual punishment, by producing poverty, disease, family distress, and untimely death.[42]

It was possible for the Christian writers of this report to explain this depravity in terms of man's innate corruption. However the reports of the Stockport Sunday School revealed a belief that the poor were not sinful simply because they were evil, but at least partly because of the impact of the environment upon their characters.

One of the elements in the social environment which the managers of the School singled out for attack was the working-class family. Parents were said to be at fault as agents of cultural transmission. They were alleged to be indifferent to their children or at worst damaging in their influence. A report of 1809 explained how the neglect of mothers and fathers affected the morality of their offspring:

> let any one walk the streets of this town, or go into the lanes and fields adjoining, and he will still be pained with the sight of numbers of poor, ragged, destitute, untaught children, spending their sabbaths in idleness and mischief. These ought to be at school, but they are unconscious of the advantages they might gain by coming, and their parents are too indifferent to *their* welfare to send them. The subscribers would be doing their

neighbours or their work-people an essential service to interfere in their behalf, and to use their influence to bring these neglected children under instruction.[43]

In addition Joseph Mayer was sufficiently concerned with the supposed depravity of parents and the counter-productive influence this entailed, to write to the major English Evangelical Sunday-school promoter, Hannah More.[44] In reply, Mrs More showed sympathy with his difficulties, affirming that the profligacy of parents affected the endeavours that she made to educate children.[45]

The promoters of the Stockport Sunday School not only indicated the ways in which parents were indifferent or counter-productive influences, they tried to provide some explanation for the failure of the working-class family. A report of 1797 drew attention to the lack of education of fathers and mothers. They had not been instructed and thus passed vices on to their children. In part, it was claimed that the economic life of the town was to blame; the high wages which a factory worker could obtain encouraged him to satisfy his immediate desires, rather than look after the welfare of his family.

> In general the labouring mechanic can obtain such wages as would if properly laid out, be a comfortable maintenance for himself and family. . . . The husband, having never been taught to relish the pleasures of domestic and social life, or those which flow from the rational and religious improvement of the mind, flies to the most sottish indulgences of sensual appetite, as the only real enjoyments in his esteem. Thus, instead of laying out his earnings in making his family comfortable, or receiving a part of them against the day of sickness or adversity, he is found sacrificing them in those brutish gratifications, which ruin the health of body and mind.[46]

In the same way, the wife and mother had not been 'instructed in the duties of her station', and had not been 'habituated to cultivate such dispositions as would diffuse happiness in her family'.[47] A report of 1811 claimed that Sunday schools were 'peculiarly well adapted' to influence the female character so that the mother's impact upon her children would no longer be negative.[48]

One element of the working environment which concerned the promoters of the Stockport Sunday School was the impact of the factory system upon the morals of the labouring poor. It is not surprising that this was the case as a majority of those educated in the

School worked in factories during the week.[49] There is some evidence which seems to indicate that the promoters were deter-mined to use their school to instruct children in habits of punctuality and work-discipline. One of the witnesses before the Commission of 1831–32, investigating the labour of children in factories, asserted that Sunday schools were 'made subservient to the disposition and will of the manufacturers, in reconciling the children to this excessive labour'. He claimed that 'almost all the lectures given are about their going from their mills to their homes, and their going from their homes to the mills. . . .'[50] However the bulk of the evidence indi-cates that, where promoters were interested in the factory system, they were concerned primarily with the personal morality of their pupils when they were at work inside the mills. They were not so interested in teaching the specific occupational virtues, which were required by industrial capitalists; this was the task of the factory master. Joseph Mayer's testimony before the Child Employment Commission of 1816 seems to support this point. He was asked: 'Have you observed that children brought up in a Sunday school are more regular in their attendance at the factories than others?' Mayer replied with an answer which implied that he considered that it was the work of the mill-owner to do this. He asserted: 'Their attendance at the factories is regulated by their master, they must attend like clock work.'[51]

In fact the references to factories in the reports of the School emphasized the need to improve the personal morality of those working inside them. A report of 1819 announced:

> What good can be expected to accrue to our people, from a few hours tuition on the Sabbath, if the beginning of the week is to usher them into accustomed scenes of the grossest wickedness? We are perfectly aware, that this is the case in many factories, where the masters are indifferent to the best interests, and careless of the moral conduct, of their work-people. . . .[52]

In fact, the managers of the School asserted that the morals of factory children could be more easily influenced inside factories than in any other kind of workplace. A report of 1807 affirmed: 'perhaps no business affords a more favourable opportunity for the maintaining of order, regularity, and good conduct, since none gives greater authority, and more constant inspection to the master. . . .'[53] In the following year, a report encouraged manufacturers to appoint moral overseers who would discourage any manifestation of immoral conduct. They would 'check every degree of impropriety, either in conversation or behaviour among those who work under their direction.'[54] In addition masters were asked to discourage all those occasions which bring the youth in their employ in company with dissipated characters, to spend their money for purposes which lead to intoxication and ultimately to disgrace and beggary.'[55] In 1814 manufacturers were advised not to employ any young people unless they availed themselves of a Sunday-school education.[56] In addition, evidence from the Child Employment Commission of 1833 indicated that factory masters were dismissing girls for immoral conduct.[57] The managers of the Stockport Sunday School, then, were primarily concerned to protect the young from the allegedly corrupting influences of factory employment, rather than to use the institution to support the economic interests of manufacturers.

The Stockport Sunday School also attacked working-class radicalism. It was not surprising that this was the case.[58] Not only were the managers of the institution members of the industrial and trading élite, who had much to lose from popular unrest, but also the Evangelical assumptions of the committee dictated that they would associate radicalism with sin. Nevertheless the managers were occasionally critical of members of their own class who often unintentially encouraged working-class unrest. The reports of the Sunday School attacked all manifestations of radicalism: political radicalism, infidelity, and trade unionism.

Subversive doctrines, the managers believed, could find a sympathetic soil in the minds of the young. In 1802 a report claimed:

> The infidel, proudly presumptuous, hides himself from the mild rays of truth, under the plausible garb of philosophy, falsely so called: he imposes his dogmas upon his youthful adherents, under the fascinating name of reason, however subversive of good order, and destructive to religion; while his unwary follower, ignorant of the consequence, and blinded by sophistry, allows himself in the gratification of every sensual pleasure, until immersed in a routine of dissipation, and whirled in a vortex of licentiousness, he glories in his shame.[59]

Infidelity then, it was alleged, undermined political stability, religion, and personal morality. Economic radicalism, the formation of trade unions, was another element that was criticized. In 1809 a report demonstrated the concern of the committee, although the failure of employers themselves was a contributory cause of their existence: 'Where the servant is treated with indifference or contempt, the master is watched with the eye of suspicion and jealousy. Hence the combinations which so much inconvenience the master, and frequently plunge the families of the workmen into irretrievable distress.'[60] More specifically, in 1812 the writers of a report attacked Luddism, although they noted that during recent disturbances the pupils of the School had not been adversely affected by this expression of discontent.[61] In 1818 and 1819 unrest in Stockport was particularly severe and several scholars and pupils were dismissed for rejecting authority inside the School. A report of 1819 asserted that Sunday schools were all the more necessary to combat the 'hydra-headed monster' of infidelity, if 'peace, happiness, truth and justice, religion and piety, are to remain amongst us'.[62] Trade unions were again attacked in a report of 1829. Referring to industrial unrest during the previous year, it claimed that, if the ideas of trade unions had been implemented, they would have subverted the foundations of society by rendering the masters the passive instrument in the hands of their servants, and eventually by banishing trade and commerce from the country, have plunged it into the most fearful and irretrievable state of misery and distress.'[63] A report of 1833 linked the Sunday school's defence of religion with that of the social order. Infidelity encouraged 'treason and rebellion' by subverting religious truth which required people 'to fear God and honour the King, and to meddle not with those who are given to change'. It attacked the 'exploded blasphemies' of the mentor of English radicalism, Thomas Paine, and it claimed in a reference to the revolutionary influence in France that every effort had been tried 'to assimilate the poorer classes' in Britain 'to the fickle and irreligious population of a neighbouring nation'. The Stockport Sunday School had not been inactive in these circumstances.

We have been labouring to impart that degree of learning and information which the increased civilization of the age renders indispensable to the lowest members of society, and endeavouring, at the same time, most anxiously to inculcate that sound religious belief and those moral habits resulting from it, without which the highest human learning is but a comparatively worthless, if not a dangerous acquisition.[64]

V

The promoters of the Stockport Sunday School believed that urban children existed in a hostile environment. They faced potential corruption from several sources, ranging from their own parents to radical agitators. They hoped that education inside the school would transform children. Instruction, they expected, would erase previously ingrained depravity.

> We believe, it will be found, that the children who have been, or are in this school, instead of singing profane or obscene songs, are heard to sing Psalms or Hymns at their work: instead of blaspheming the name of the God who made them, they speak with reverence of the Almighty: instead of speaking falsehoods, they have learnt to speak the truth: instead of wishing to run off from their work to any idle sports, they are generally found diligent and attentive to their various employments.[65]

Religion formed the basis of this education; it taught men

> to understand the mild tenor of those laws by which they are governed, they will discern in them a train of justice and equity not to be excelled; – becoming acquainted with those sacred oracles, which teach them to render 'fear to whom fear, and honor to whom honor is due'; they will regard with the highest reverence that admirable mechanism, which links together the various classes of society, and start with abhorrence from the idea, that would in the slightest degree disorganize its beauty or disturb its regularity.[66]

The promoters and managers of the Stockport Sunday School offered to solve the problems created by urban society. Evangelical and conservative images combated the influence of depravity in an attempt to establish a new pattern of spiritual and social harmony.

NOTES

1 This interpretation is presented in M. M. Dick 'English Conservatives and Schools for the Poor *c.* 1780–1833: a study of the Sunday School, School of Industry and the Philanthrophic Society's School for Vagrant and Criminal Children' (unpublished Ph.D. thesis, University of Leicester, 1979).

2 On Chalmers see Laurance James Saunders, *Scottish Democracy 1815–1840* (Edinburgh, 1950), pp. 208–21; Trygve R. Tholfsen, *Working Class Radicalism in Mid Victorian England* (1976), pp. 37–9.

3 Thomas Chalmers, *On the Advantages of Local Sabbath Schools* (Glasgow, 1824).

4 Ibid., p. 85.

5 W. I. Wild, *The History of the Stockport Sunday School* ... (1891), p. 3. Thomas Walter Laqueur, *Religion and Respectability: Sunday Schools and Working Class Culture 1780–1850* (1976), p. 64.

6 The most detailed history of Stockport is Phyllis M. Giles, 'Economic and social development of Stockport 1815–1836 (unpublished M.A. thesis, University of Manchester, 1950), 3 vols. This should be supplemented by Henry Heginbotham, *Stockport, Ancient and Modern* (1892), 2 vols. I. J. Steele, 'A survey of the education of the working class in Stockport during the nineteenth century' (unpublished M.A. thesis, University of Sheffield, 1967), contains much relevant material on the social and economic context of the Stockport Sunday School.

7 Giles, op. cit., vol. i, pp. 45–6; Steele, op. cit., p. 6; William Astle, *History of Stockport* (Stockport, 1971), reprint of 1922 edition, pp. 18–19. For Marsland's membership of the committee see Stockport Reference Library (St. R. L.), SK 52, Stockport Sunday School Reports 1806–1825, Annual Report 1815, p. 15.

8 Astle, op. cit., p. 16.

9 R. Price Williams, 'On the Increase of Population in England and Wales', *Journal of the Statistical Society*, vol. xliii (September 1880), p. 486.

10 St. R. L., SK 52, Reports 1806–25, op. cit., Annual Report 1806, pp. 27–9.

11 Heginbotham, op. cit., vol. i, p. 74.

12 Ibid., loc. cit.

13 Ibid., vol. i, pp. 73, 75–7, 93–8; Steele, op. cit., pp. 11, 12, 21, 33.

14 Giles, op. cit., vol. i, pp. 124–5; Heginbotham, op. cit., vol. i, pp. 76–7, 82, 84, 94–6; Steele, op. cit., pp. 34–6.

15 Heginbotham, op. cit., vol. i, p. 77.

16 Ibid., pp. 76–7.

17 Giles, op. cit., vol. i, pp. 124–234, vol. ii, pp. 336–425.

18 Steele, op. cit., p. 34; Heginbotham, op. cit., vol. i, p. 82.

19 Giles, op. cit., vol. i, p. 124; Heginbotham, op. cit., p. 75.

20 Ibid., pp. 75–7.

21 Ibid., p. 75.

22 Steele, op. cit., p. 35. For Prescott see Giles, op. cit., vol. i, p. 83.

23 Heginbotham, op. cit., vol. i, pp. 77–82.

24 Giles, op. cit., vol. i, pp. 182–4, vol. ii, p. 514.

25 Heginbotham, op. cit., vol. i, pp. 82–3.

26 Donald Read, *Peterloo, The Massacre and its Background* (Manchester, 1958), reprint of 1973 edn, pp. 47–8.

27 Heginbotham, op. cit., vol. i, p. 84.

28 Ibid., pp. 184–8.

29 Ibid., pp. 89–90.

30 Ibid., pp. 93–5.

31 Ibid., p. 96.

32 Astle, op. cit., p. 20.

33 Wild, op. cit., pp. 3–4.

34 Steele, op. cit., p. 23. Mayer was the son of a cotton manufacturer, he became the first General Inspector of the Stockport Sunday School between 1806 and 1815, and was later to act as Treasurer, ibid., pp. 166–9; Heginbotham, op. cit., vol. ii, p. 397; St. R. L., SK 52, Reports 1806–25, op. cit., Annual Report 1821, p. 13.

35 Wild, op. cit., p. xxxi.

36 Steele, op. cit., pp. 17, 18–19, 166–8; E. P. Thompson, *The Making of the English Working Class* (Harmondsworth, 1968), pp. 385–91, 412–13.

37 Laqueur, op. cit., p. 196.

38 A list of committee members for 1815–16 and 1821–22 are in St. R. L., SK 52, Reports 1806–25, op. cit., Annual Reports 1815, p. 15, and 1821, p. 13. The proportion was obtained by checking the names of committee members against lists in *The Commercial Directory for 1816–17, containing the Names, Trades and Situations of the Merchants, Manufacturers, Tradesmen, etc. in Ashton, Barnsley and Birmingham* . . . (Manchester, 1816), pp. 321–8, and *Pigot and Dean's New Directory of Manchester, Salford etc., for 1821–22* (Manchester, n.d.), pp. 323–32.

39 St. R. L., B/S/2/18, Stockport Sunday School Annual Reports of the Methodist Sunday School 1794–1804, Annual Report 1795, p. 2.

40 St. R. L., B/S/2/18, Reports 1794–1804, Annual Report 1796, p. 1.

41 St. R. L., B/S/2/18, Reports 1794–1804, Annual Report 1802, p. 1.

42 Ibid., pp. 1–2.

43 St. R. L., SK 52, Reports 1806–25, op. cit., Annual Report 1809, p. 1.

44 Two letters from Hannah More, written in reply to correspondence from Joseph Mayer, are held by St. R. L., B/S/52, Stockport Sunday School Letters 1795–1810.

45 Ibid., Hannah More to Joseph Mayer 15 July 1795.

46 St. R. L., B/S/2/18, Reports 1794–1804, op. cit., Annual Report 1797, p. 1.

47 Ibid., loc. cit.

48 St. R. L., SK 52, Reports 1806–25, op. cit., Annual Report 1811, p. 6.

49 *Supplementary Reports from Commissioners appointed to collect information in the manufacturing districts, relative to the Employment of Children in Factories . . . with Minutes of Evidence and Reports of District Commissioners* 1834 (167) xx, Returns relating to the Stockport Sunday School, pp. 158–9.

50 *Report from the Select Committee to whom the Bill to regulate the labour of children in mills and factories of the United Kingdom was referred* 1831–2 (706) xv, p. 281.

51 *Report of the Select Committee on the State of children employed in the*

Manufactories of the United Kingdom . . . with Minutes of Evidence . . . 1816 (397) iii, p. 54.

52 St. R. L., SK 52, Reports 1806–25, op. cit., Annual Report 1819, p. 11.

53 St. R. L., SK 52, Reports 1806–25, op. cit., Annual Report 1807, p. 6.

54 St. R. L., SK 52, Reports 1806–25, op. cit., Annual Report 1808, p. 11.

55 Ibid., pp. 11–12.

56 St. R. L., SK 52, Reports 1806–25, op. cit., Annual Report 1814, p. 5.

57 *First Report of the Commissioners appointed to collect information in the manufacturing districts relative to the Employment of Children in Factories . . . with Minutes of Evidence and Reports of District Commissioners* 1833 (450) xx. Examinations taken by Mr Cowell, D. I. Stockport, p. 86.

58 Laqueur argues that the managers of the Stockport Sunday School were not interested in the politics of its teachers and pupils, Laqueur op. cit., pp. 193, 196–9, 200. This interpretation is questioned in Dick, op. cit., ch. 4.

59 St. R. L., B/S/2/18, Reports 1794–1804, op. cit., Annual Report 1802, p. 2.

60 St. R. L., SK 52, Reports 1806–25, op. cit., Annual Report 1809, p. 10.

61 St. R. L., SK 52, Reports 1806–25, op. cit., Annual Report 1812, pp. 7–8.

62 St. R. L., SK 52, Reports 1806–25, op. cit., Annual Report 1819, pp. 6–8.

63 St. R. L., SK 52, Stockport Sunday School Reports 1826–47, Annual Report 1829, p. 8.

64 St. R. L., SK 52, Reports 1826–47, op. cit., Annual Report, 1833, pp. 4–5.

65 St. R. L., B/S/2/18, Reports 1794–1804, op. cit., Annual Report, 1795, p. 2.

66 St. R. L., SK 52, Reports 1806–25, op. cit., Annual Report 1817, p. 5.

The Sunday School
in Nineteenth-Century Literature:
An Exploration

Colin Riches

The sources available for the study of English Sunday schools are vast. There is a rich store of primary[1] and secondary material ranging from the manuscript letters of Robert Raikes to an extensive stock of printed books, pamphlets, and ephemera, which is still being added to today, but not with the same rapidity as in the nineteenth century. Raikes was skilled in recording and publicizing Sunday-school activities and his place in the history of the movement is assured because of this. Newby has written that he is 'the father of the Sunday School not as its inventor, still less as its maker or perfector but as its prophet';[2] he could have added 'its publicist'. A typical letter is the one he wrote to the Revd M. Price of Coln Rogers, near Northleach:

My dear Sir, It gave me great pleasure to hear from you. I have enclosed you a copy of a letter which the innumerable applications from all Parts of the Kingdom compelled me to print. This gives the general outline, but the Reformation must arise from a steady pursuit of that Trait in our Blessed Redeemer's Character – *He went about.* I go round the houses of the Poor. Enquire how the children behave – make the wicked disobedient kneel down and beg Pardon of their Parents. Point out to them how greatly it is within their own Power to improve their situations and increase their Happiness and Comforts by such a Behaviour as well as establish good character. By this means the People tell me that my name keeps more decorum than all their —— could effect. The Deserving I reward with books or some article of Cloathes and a pair of shoes . . . . I have lately brought to a constant Attendance at early Prayers, Boys who were persecutors of their companions who had adopted the Practice; they were ridiculing others, laughing at and calling them names for coming to Church and now came with great regularity themselves . . .[3]

By letters such as these to newspapers and private individuals Robert Raikes has built up for us a graphic (although at times slightly contradictory picture) of how he recruited for and organized his Sunday schools; later chroniclers were not so skilled. In spite of all that has been written about the virtues, vices, and vicissitudes of the movement well-observed and close descriptions of the minute-by-minute happenings in a Sunday school are disappointingly rare. But as a result of the frustration arising from this dearth of human detail, this researcher has, like others before him, turned to literary sources as possible avenues of information, encouraged initially by reading in all its colour and richness the Sunday-school scene as described by Arnold Bennett (1867–1931) in *Clayhanger*.[4] The search to date through a large store of nineteenth-century literary sources has been interesting but not yet as yielding as Bennett's work and in that sense the inquiry has also been somewhat frustrating. Robert Woolf has written that 'of all the subjects that interested Victorians, and therefore preoccupied their novelists, none – not love, or crime, or war, or sport, or ancestry, or even money – held their attention as much as religion.'[5] For some reason Sunday schools did not have the same fascination and indeed in many novels of that period religion itself is far from a central concern. *Wives and Daughters* by Elizabeth Gaskell (1810–65) is a case in point: in this novel 'religion in any obvious form virtually disappears. While in her previous work one recognized that churchgoing was no part of the life of Mary Bart's mill workers, nor of the isolated dwellers Sylvia Robson and her family, it is astonishing, in a novel like *Wives and Daughters*, wholly working through day to day activities and unsensational events, that the organized religion which necessarily formed a regular, even routine, part of them is given only the slightest mention.'[6]

Even when there is a religious theme Sunday schools are pushed into the background. For example a close reading of *Salem Chapel* (1863), a full-length novel by Mrs Margaret Oliphant (1828–97), which is centred around the life of a Dissenting congregation and their new minister, reveals only two oblique references to Sunday schools. Mr Tufton, the former minister, tells his successor, Arthur Vincent, that 'the sermon to the children' by themselves once a year is important. 'My plan has been to take the congregation in classes; the young men – ah! and they're especially important are the young men.' At another point in the story we are informed that the schoolroom 'once intended for a school but never used except on Sundays in that capacity' has been decorated for a new meeting. Some manufactured festoons of evergreens, some concocted pink and white roses in paper to embellish the same. The printed texts of the Sunday school were framed and in some cases obliterated in Christmas garlands.[7] One would have thought it difficult to write about chapel life with virtually no reference to Sunday schools but such is the case in this novel and those by other minor novelists like Mrs Trollope (1780–1863), mother of Anthony Trollope, and Elizabeth Sewell (1815–1906) who manage to deal in depth with Anglican clergy, their causes and conflicts, without even hinting at the existence of Sunday schools in the parishes which their characters people.

By now it will be apparent that we have interpreted the term 'literature' very widely. It includes all writing produced for purposes different from mere factual description and springing from inspiration rather than knowledge although (as we shall see) it can be grounded in fact and represent a world which is more real than say – in this context – the minute books of a Sunday school or a government inquiry which produces statistics and/or written or oral evidence relating to Sunday schools. We are not therefore confining our inquiry to the major novelists of the nineteenth century but are extending it to mention representatives of the minor novelists writing for both adults and children. Fiction which has Sunday-school life as integral to the narrative appears to be largely confined to pamphlets and tracts in the shape of stories intended for younger readers. However, references to Sunday schools as a setting for narrative incidents are more frequent although surprisingly limited. Maybe this incomplete exploration has failed to unearth a rich seam of Sunday-school themes but so far the yield has been valuable but thin.

While the existing factual material on Sunday schools is limited and there is a paucity of literary sources the use of literary material in historical exegesis may impose further limitations. This is part of a wider debate in historiography on how best to recover the lives and times of ordinary people, if one argues that the pivot of history is not the uncommon but the usual, and the true makers of history are 'the people'. How does one discover the commonplace experiences of ordinary men and women of the past as distinct from the presumed spokesmen of traditional history? The documents of personal history such as diaries, journals, commonplace books, personal correspondence, and fictional material 'provide subjective commentary on events, interpret experiences, preserve facts and express feelings according to some personal sense of what is meaningful and they communicate an intense understanding of what one's own life is and has been.' Of course the coverage of this type of material is enormous – descriptive, narrative, exploratory, interpretive, analytical, and critical and the quality is equally varied from the tedious to dramatic, lucid to obscure, naive to sophisticated, unconscious to self conscious'.[8]

The limited use of such documents in social history is partly explained by their inaccessibility, the labour of separating the dross from the gold and their supposed excessive subjectivity and unrepresentativeness. Moreover, written sources only give us the perspectives of the literate, and the illiterate have no voice here. Clearly by their very nature these sources are idiosyncratic to some extent but they do provide perspectives of reality which scholars in the humanities and social sciences are turning their attention to.[9] However the approach is not without its critics among Marxists and others who argue that this emphasis on the significance of personal and interpersonal experience often fails to take into account how structural constraints shape individual perceptions of reality. Widdowson *et al.* (1979) contend that literature, which is in essence a record of personal reality, cannot be a neutral category hiding behind notions like 'taste', 'sensibility', 'intelligence', and tradition as if it was morally uncommitted when in fact it has a heavy 'ideological function'.[10]

However, there is a similar danger of hiding behind some sort of structural view of the world and finding the facts to fit the case. Johnson[11] has unsuccessfully attempted to explain the growth of Sunday schools in terms of capitalist domination and by so doing has ignored the many individual motives which inspired them. These types of argument do not detract from the value of the phenomenological approach, but merely point to the possible origins of different perceptions found in literature and elsewhere.

This brings us to the special case of literature as a reliable historical source. Chedzoy has recently contended that there is a strong case to be made for what he calls 'fictional truth' as an account of reality: if literature is not literally true it may reveal a deeper truth; it does provide a type of knowledge of a unique kind; and in any case it makes no pretence to be factual – the literary person never 'maketh any circles about your imagination to conjure you to believe for true what he writes'.[12] The respective value of primary, autobiographical, and literary sources can be illustrated from Bennett's coverage of Sunday schools in *Clayhanger*, the autobiographical material of Charles Shaw in *When I was a Child*,[13] and the limited manuscript material available.

Charles Shaw was born in Tunstall in 1832 and went to the Sunday school of the Methodist New Connexion there. The general history of this denomination is well documented.[14] As for Sunday schools we know that in 1831 there were nine in Hanley Circuit (which included Tunstall) with 400 superintendents and teachers (of whom only 178 were members of the 'Society') and 2,460 scholars. The minutes of the MNC record the concerns of the Connexion in regard to their Sunday schools in the nineteenth century, including worries that the control of the schools was slipping away from the minister and they were losing their evangelical zeal, and by the end of the century they were alarmed at the decrease in scholars.[15] Primary information on the MNC Sunday school at Tunstall is very thin. Goldstraw[16] relies on Shaw's account for his documentation. Other primary sources on Sunday schools in Staffordshire include the Appendix to the Final Report of the Commissioners (Mines) (1842), when James Mitchell records details about Sunday schools in the South Staffordshire Coalfield, and the valuable independent comments of deputations from the Sunday School Union in London who visited the area from time to time. For example in 1846 the Sunday schools in the Newcastle-under-Lyme and Burslem Union (of which the Tunstall and neighbourhood branch formed a part) were visited by Mr Mason, Secretary, and Mr Cuthbertson, who reported (among other things) that writing was taught in some schools 'as an inducement for them [the scholars] to remain'; most of the elementary instruction was given through the Sunday schools; evening meetings could not be held because of the engagement of the young people in the factories and 'some Sunday schools had large libraries but the books were very little read'.[17] The material we have here may be valuable but it is very basic and not always explicit.

'The Old Potter' is much more vivid and detailed in his recall of events. Besides attending 'Betty's' dame school he 'concurrently' went to Sunday school and had been well prepared, because by that time he could read so that he was put in the Bible Class at the age of six. The school was held in the main body of the chapel. Shaw continues:

> One day I remember the superintendent of the Sunday school, Daniel Spilsbury, came to the class in which I was sitting, and called me out. He took me to the staircase leading up into the gallery of the chapel (for in the body of this chapel our Sunday school was held). We sat down on the stairs, and he gave me a Bible and told me to read certain passages. I did so. The old man smiled pleasantly upon me, and stroking my hair, he told me to be a good boy, and said, the Bible I had read from (an old one without backs) I could take home as a present. Sunday school prizes had not then come into fashion. I may say here I never remember any difficulty in reading or spelling, except, of course, very exceptional and long words in the Bible. We had spelling in our Sunday school in the afternoon, and in my class we had words up to five syllables, but I managed to trip them off easily, while other boys struggled and scowled at their spelling books as if they hated the sight of them. The praise of my success I give to old Betty's method of teaching. But what shall I say of the benefit I got from the Sunday school? To speak of the benefit it has been to this nation would be a joy, and all I could say would fail to tell the measure of its beneficence and inspiration, especially to the children of the poor in those days. To me, very soon, it was a life within my life. In the midst of a life of hardship and temptation, this inner life shed a brightness and a sweetness which always gave me an upward look and an upward aspiration. Sunday was verily an oasis in the desert to me. Whatever the weather on other days, Sunday always seemed to me a sun's day. It gave me the only gladsome morning of the week. I got a washing that morning such as I had not time to get on other mornings. I had poor enough clothing to put on, but my eldest sister always helped me in my toilet on Sunday morning, and my hair got brushed and combed and oiled (with scented oil), so that I always carried a fragrance with me. I have the memory of that scent yet, and when I meet with it since, I know it in a moment. With this fragrance I always had the feeling of flowers about me.[18]

The passage has been quoted at length because it was drawn upon heavily by Arnold Bennett (and unacknowledged for some time) in *Clayhanger*.

73

The days at Tunall (Tunstall?) Sunday school, and particularly the superintendent, had made a deep impression on the mind and life of Darius Clayhanger. Edwin, his son, believed that he had 'a superstitious and hypocritical regard for the Sunday schools. Darius never went near the Sunday school and assuredly in business and in home life he did not practise the precept inculcated at the Sunday school and yet he always spoke of the Sunday school with what was to Edwin a ridiculous reverence.'[19] Earlier in the novel we find a passage which is closely paralleled to Shaw's recall:

> Upon hearing that Darius was going out into the world the superintendent of the Sunday school, a grave whiskered young man of perhaps thirty, led him one morning out of the body of the primitive Methodist chapel which served as a schoolroom before and after chapel service, up into the deserted gallery of the chapel, and then seated him on a stair and knelt on the stair below him, and caressed his head, and called him a good boy, and presented him with an old battered Bible. This volume was the most valuable thing that Darius had ever possessed. He ran all the way home with it, half suffocated by his triumph. Sunday school prizes had not then been invented. The young superintendent of the Sunday School was Mr Shushions.[20]

For Darius such was the attraction of the Sunday school that he was there the next morning with scented hair two minutes before the opening. What Edwin did not know until much later was that Darius, a pauper boy, had been rescued by the superintendent and given a new start in life. At one time Shaw had been to the workhouse and had experienced many horrors there. His Sunday-school education had enabled him to become a local preacher and eventually a minister of the Methodist New Connexion; through Sunday school he was able (to use Bennett's phrase) 'to plunge into the river of intellectual life'. What happened to his revered teacher George Kirkham we do not know but Bennett gives a vivid and moving picture of the fate of Mr Shushions.

Shortly before his death the old superintendent had attempted to gain a seat on the platform at the Bursley (Burslem?) Sunday school centenary celebrations as

'. . . th'oldest Sunday-school teacher i th' Five Towns. Aye! Fifty years and more since I was Super at Turnhill Primitive

Sunday schoo', and all Turnhill knows on it. And I've got to get on that there platform. I'm th' oldest Sunday-schoo' teacher i th' Five Towns. And I was Super –'

Two ribald youngsters intoned 'Super, Super,' and another person unceremoniously jammed the felt hat on the old man's head.

'It's nowt to me if ye was forty Supers,' said the policeman, with menacing disdain. 'I've got my orders, and I'm not here to be knocked about. Where did ye have yer last drink?'

'No wine, no beer, nor spirit-uous liquors have I tasted for sixty-one years come Martinmas,' whimpered the old man. And he gave another lurch against the policeman. 'My name's Shushions!' And he repeated in a frantic treble, 'My name's Shushions!'

'Go and bury thysen, owd gaffer!' a Herculean young collier advised him.[21]

Hilda Lessways persuaded Edwin Clayhanger to use his authority to satisfy the old man's wishes.

Thus was the doddering old fool who had given his youth to Sunday school when Sunday schools were not patronized by princes, archbishops, and lord mayors, when Sunday schools were the scorn of the intelligent, and had sometimes to be held in public-houses for lack of better accommodation, – thus was he taken off for a show and a museum curiosity by indulgent and shallow Samaritans who had not even the wit to guess that he had sown what they were reaping. And Darius Clayhanger stood oblivious at a high window of the sacred Bank. And Edwin, who, all unconscious, owed the very fact of his existence to the doting imbecile, regarded him chiefly as a figure in a tableau, as the chance instrument of a woman's beautiful revelation. Mr Shushions's sole crime against society was that he had forgotten to die.[22]

These are poignant words about Sunday schools (which were to wane in numbers attending within thirty years or so)[23] and about the great impact Sunday schools had had on individual lives and ironically – although coincidentally – Robert Shaw's last days had some similarity to Mr Shushions'.

Clayhanger was published in 1900; in 1906 'due to old age and inability to work Shaw died in poverty. . . .' Fact and fiction became almost inextricably linked.

We return now to consider the value of these various sources. Shaw's inaccuracies were certainly repeated by Bennett. Sunday-school prizes were in fashion in the 1830s. Robert Raikes, as we have seen, issued them. However, Gillian Avery observes that only books 'with their gilt and pictorial covers really suggest prizes' and not the earlier, drab little tracts, measuring about four and one-eighth by two and three-quarter inches, very often only paper-covered 'which were given as prizes but were more frequently distributed to poor homes by parish workers'.[24] The 1850s and 1860s were the golden years for the amateur writer of advisory and exhortatory tales for favoured Sunday school scholars; after the 1870 Education Act these reward books served two markets and became more informative and less religious in tone. So the inaccuracy here, for example, may not be as great as it may seem on the surface. In any case Bennett captures a quality in his writing which is not present in any of the sources listed. Literature is not the only authority but it is one authority.

Another example of 'fictional truth' is the description in *Clay-hanger* of the Sunday School Centenary Celebration at Bursley. Bennett probably witnessed the celebrations at Burslem; the wealth of detail certainly suggests that this was so. The turn out in the pottery towns was one of many celebrations throughout the country. The 1879 Report of the SSU records that about £25,000 was to be spent and a commemorative medal would be struck and engraved 'Scholars Receipts' [*sic*] with a portrait of Raikes. Eventually 789,956 medals were sold![25] The Centenary Week began in the metropolis on Monday, 28 June 1880, with the opening of the Centenary Convention at the Guildhall when the SSI, the Committee of Methodist Union, and the Ragged School Union united with the SSU. Throughout the week 'a religious influence was felt and holy passions were stirred': Wednesday was Children's Day at the Crystal Palace: on the Friday evening a communion service was presided over by C. H. Spurgeon at which two to three thousand people were present. On 3 July Raikes's statue was unveiled in the Embankment Gardens by Lord Shaftesbury and others and in the afternoon of that day a grand concert was held in the Albert Hall. *The Times* reported twenty-nine capital and provincial events in the space of a month. On 23 June a letter to that paper referred to the fact that each child was being asked to contribute one penny for a prayer book for the daughters of Her Royal Highness the Princess of Wales and the writer calculated that for 20,000 children this would be £83 6s. for three prayer books!

Burslem's celebrations do not get a mention in *The Times* but Bennett has served the town better with a much more powerful picture than any newspaper could produce. There is first the formation and marching of processions towards St Luke's Square:

> The band blared; the crimson cheeks of the trumpeters sucked in and out; the drummer leaned backwards to balance his burden, and banged. Every soul of the variegated company, big and little, was in a perspiration. The staggering bearers of the purple banner, who held the great poles in leathern sockets slung from the shoulders, and their acolytes before and behind who kept the banner upright by straining at crimson halyards, sweated most of all. Every foot was grey with dust, and the dark trousers of boys and men showed dust. The steamy whiff of humanity struck Edwin's nostrils. Up hill and down dale the procession had already walked two miles. Yet it was alert, joyous, and expectant: a chattering procession. From the lorry rose a continuous faint shriek of infantile voices. Edwin was saddened as by pathos. I believe that as he gazed at the procession waggling away along Wedgwood street he saw Sunday schools in a new light.
>
> And that was the opening of the day. There were to be dozens of such processions. Some would start only in the town itself; but others were coming from the villages like Red Cow, five sultry miles off.[26]

Later the bustle of people, spectators, and participants is described:

> As the police cordon closed on the procession from the Old Church, definitely dividing the spectators from the spectacle, it grew clear that the spectators were in the main a shabby lot; persons without any social standing: unkempt idlers, good-for-nothings, wastrels, clay-whitened pot-girls who had to work even on that day, and who had run out for a few moments in their flannel aprons to stare, and a few score ragamuffins, whose parents were too poor or too careless to make them superficially presentable enough to figure in a procession. Nearly the whole respectability of the town was either fussily marshalling processions or gazing

down at them in comfort from the multitudinous open windows of the square. The 'leads' over the projecting windows of Baines's, the chief draper's were crowded with members of the ruling caste.

And even within the Square, it could be seen, between the towering backs of constables, that the spectacle itself was chiefly made up of indigence bedecked. The thousands of perspiring children, penned like sheep, and driven to and fro, like sheep by anxious and officious rosettes, nearly all had the air of poverty decently putting the best face on itself; they were nearly all, beneath their vague sense of importance, wistful with the resigned fatalism of the young and of the governed. They knew not precisely why they were there; but merely that they had been commanded to be there, and that they were hot and thirsty, and that for weeks they had been learning hymns by heart for this occasion, and that the occasion was glorious.

The whole square was now suddenly revealed as a swarming mass of heads, out of which rose banners and pennons that were cruder in tint even than the frocks and hats of the little girls and the dresses and bonnets of their teachers; the men, too, by their neckties, scarves, and rosettes, added colour. All the windows were chromatic with the hues of bright costumes, and from many windows and from every roof that had a flagstaff flags waved heavily against the gorgeous sky. At the bottom of the Square the lorries with infants had been arranged, and each looked like a bank of variegated flowers. The principal bands – that is to say, all the bands that could be trusted – were collected round the red baize platform at the top of the Square, and the vast sun-reflecting euphoniums, trumpets, and cornets made a glittering circle about the officials and ministers and their wives and women. All denominations, for one day only, fraternized effusively together on that platform; for princes of the royal house, and the Archbishop of Canterbury and the Lord Mayor of London had urged that it should be so. The Primitive Methodists' parson discovered himself next but one to Father Milton, who on any other day would have been a Popish priest, and whose wooden substitute for a wife was the queen on a chessboard. And on all these the sun blazed torridly.[27]

We are given details of one Sunday-school banner emblazoned with 'The Blood of the Lamb', of the crushing force of the singing and playing of 'Rock of Ages', and then the prayer 'Oh most merciful Lord; Have pity on us, We are brands plucked from the burning', all males baring their heads except for the policemen who 'by virtue of their high office, could dare to affront the majesty of God'. It is a closely observed account, well balanced, and in places sympathetic to Sunday schools.

In *Anna of the Five Towns* (1902), where the plot is set more closely in a Sunday-school context with Titus Price the Senior Superintendent meeting his debts by stealing from the chapel and eventually committing suicide, there is an equally sympathetic portrait of Sunday-school life – the prize-giving, the special teachers' meeting, the bazaar with the grand Sunday-school stall and the long account of the Sunday-school treat with its games and tea where teachers are set apart from the scholars.[28]

The school-treat was held in a twelve-acre field near Sneyd, the seat of a marquis, and a Saturday afternoon resort very popular in the Five Towns. The children were formed at noon on Duck Bank into a procession, which marched to the railway station to the singing of 'Shall we gather at the river?' Thence a special train carried them, in seething compartments, excited and strident, to Sneyd, where the procession was reformed along a country road. There had been two sharp showers in the morning, and the vacillating sky threatened more rain; but because the sun had shone dazzlingly at eleven o'clock all the women and girls, too easily tempted by the glory of the moment, blossomed forth in pale blouses and parasols. The chattering crowd, bright and defenceless as flowers, made at Sneyd a picture at once gay and pathetic. It had rained there at half-past twelve; the roads were wet; and among the two hundred and fifty children and thirty teachers there were less than a score umbrellas.

On arrival at Sneyd the more conscientious teachers set themselves seriously to the task of amusing the smaller children, and the smaller children consented to be amused according to the recipes appointed by long custom for school-treats. Many round-games, which invariably comprised singing or kissing, being thus annually resuscitated by elderly people from the deeps of memory, were preserved for a posterity which otherwise would never have known them. Among these was Bobby-Bingo. For twenty-five years Titus Price had played at Bobby-Bingo with the infant classes at the school-treat, and this year he was bound by the expectations of all to continue the practice. Another diversion which he always took care to organize was the three-legged race for boys. Also, he usually joined in the tut-ball, a quaint game which owes its surprising longevity to the fact that it is equally proper for both sexes. Within half an hour the treat was in full career; football, cricket, rounders, tick, leap-frog, prison-bars, and round-games, transformed the field into a vast arena of complicated struggles and emulations. All were occupied, except a few of the women and older girls, who strolled languidly about in the *rôle* of spectators.

The treat ended disastrously. In the middle of the children's meal, while, yet the enormous double-handled tea-cans were being carried up and down the thirsty rows, and the boys were causing their bags to explode with appalling detonations, it began to rain sharply. The fickle sun withdrew his splendour from the toilettes, and was seen no more for a week afterwards. 'It's come at last', ejaculated Mynors, who had watched the sky with anxiety for an hour previously. He mobilized the children and ranked them under a row of elms. The teachers, running to the tent for their own tea, said to one another that the shower could only be a brief one. The wish was father to the thought, for they were a little ashamed to be under cover while their charges precariously sheltered beneath dripping trees – yet there was nothing else to be done; the men took turns in the rain to keep the children in their places. The sky was completely overcast. 'It's set in for a wet evening, and so we may as well make the best of it', Beatrice said grimly, and she sent the landau home empty. She was right. A forlorn and disgusted snake of a procession crawled through puddles to the station. The platform resounded with sneezes. None but a dressmaker could have discovered a silver lining to the black and all-pervading cloud which had ruined so many dozens of fair costumes. Anna, melancholy and taciturn, exerted herself to minimize the discomfort of her scholars.[29]

Charlotte Brontë (1816–55) in *Shirley* (1849) has a more marked age and social division in the Whit-Tuesday Sunday-school 'Feast' held at Briarfield when the twelve hundred scholars from that parish, Whenbury, and Hummelly were assembled together for their treat in the schoolrooms.

.. twenty tables each calculated to accommodate twenty guests, were laid out, surrounded with benches, and covered with white cloths: above them were suspended at least some twenty cages, containing as many canaries, according to a fancy of the district, specially cherished by Mr Helstone's clerk who delighted in the piercing song of these birds, and knew that amidst confusion of tongues they always carolled loudest. These tables, be it understood, were not spread for the twelve hundred scholars to be assembled from the three parishes, but only for the patrons and teachers of the schools: the children's feast was to be spread in the open air. At one o'clock the troops were to come in; at two they were to be marshalled; till four they were to parade the parish; then came the feast, and afterwards the meeting, with music and speechifying in the church.[30]

Another divisive element in Sunday schools hinted at by Bennett was the denominational one which affected Sunday-school affairs throughout the nineteenth century. The Sunday School Society (1785) with a committee consisting of equal numbers of Anglicans and Nonconformists was followed by the establishment of the SSU in 1803 which was intended to be interdenominational but in practice had a major appeal to the Nonconformist denominations.

In 1843 the Sunday School Institute, a distinctly Church of England organization, was set up. The Unitarians had their own society as did other denominations and in 1880 were lamenting the fact that they had wanted to join the Church of England and other denominations in the centenary celebrations 'but their place was not recognized among the Christian communities'.[31]

At Briarfield the scene was set for a physical confrontation, at what was intended as a delight for the children, between the Nonconformists and Anglicans. As the latter's procession marched towards their rendezvous so the opposition came in the opposite direction. Helstone, the senior minister, complained.

> 'The Dissenting and Methodist schools, the Baptists, Independents, and Wesleyans, joined in unholy alliance, and turning purposely into this lane with the intention of obstructing our march and driving us back.'
> 'Bad manners!' said Shirley; 'and I hate bad manners. Of course, they must have a lesson.'

'A lesson in politeness,' suggested Mr Hall, who was ever for peace: 'not an example of rudeness.'

Old Helstone moved on. Quickening his step, he marched some yards in advance of his company. He had nearly reached the other sable leaders, when he who appeared to act as the hostile commander-in-chief – a large, greasy man, with black hair combed flat on his forehead – called a halt. The procession paused: he drew forth a hymn-book, gave out a verse, set a tune, and they all struck up the most dolorous of canticles.

Helstone signed to his bands: they clashed out with all the power of brass. He desired them to play 'Rule, Britannua', and ordered the children to join in vocally, which they did with enthusiastic spirit. The enemy was sung and stormed down; his psalm quelled: as far as noise went, he was conquered.

'Now, follow me!' exclaimed Helstone: 'not at a run, but at a firm, smart pace. Be steady, every child and woman of you: – keep together – hold on by each other's skirts, if necessary.'

They drove on regardless and clashed with the Nonconformists.

The fat Dissenter who had given out the hymn was left sitting in the ditch. He was a spirit merchant by trade, a leader of the Nonconformists, and, it was said, drank more water in that one afternoon than he had swallowed for a twelve-month before. Mr Hall had taken care of Caroline, and Caroline of him: he and Miss Ainley made their own quiet comments to each other afterwards on the incident. Miss Keeldar and Mr Helstone shook hands heartily when they had fairly got the whole party through the lane. The curates began to exult, but Mr Helstone presently put the curb on their innocent spirits: he remarked that they never had sense to know what to say, and had better hold their tongues, and he reminded them that the business was none of their managing.

About half-past three the procession turned back, and at four once more regained the starting-place. Long lines of benches were arranged in the close-shorn fields round the school: there the children were seated, and huge baskets, covered up with white cloths, and great smoking tin vessels were brought out. Ere the distribution of good things commenced, a brief grace was pronounced by Mr Hall, and sung by the children: their young voices sounded melodious, even touching, in the open air. Large currant buns, and hot, well-sweetened tea, were then administered in the proper spirit of liberality: no stinting was permitted on this day, at least; the rule for each child's allowance being that it was to have about twice as much as it could possibly eat, thus leaving a reserve to be carried home for such as age, sickness, or other impediment, prevented from coming to the feast. Buns and beer circulated, meantime, amongst the musicians and church-singers: afterwards the benches were removed, and they were left to unbend their spirits in licensed play.

A bell summoned the teachers, patrons, and patronesses to the schoolroom; Miss Keeldar, Miss Helstone, and many other ladies were already there, glancing over the arrangement of their separate trays and tables. Most of the female servants of the neighbourhood, together with the clerks', the singers', and the musicians' wives, had been pressed into the service of the day as waiters: each vied with the other in smartness and daintiness of dress, and many handsome forms were seen amongst the younger ones. About half a score were cutting bread and butter; another half-score supplying hot water, brought from the coppers of the Rector's kitchen. The profusion of flowers and evergreens decorating the white walls, the show of silver teapots and bright porcelain on the tables, the active figures, blithe faces, gay dresses flitting about everywhere, formed altogether a refreshing and lively spectacle. Everybody talked, not very loudly, but merrily, and the canary birds sang shrill in their high-hung cages.[32]

This is an event well told. (It will be noted that the Temperance Movement had not yet influenced Sunday-school treats; indeed in the early days cakes and ale were quite common as a celebration.) One regrets that neither Charlotte nor her sisters wrote more on the subject of Sunday schools. They were daughters of the parsonage, steeped in the Evangelical Revival which gave impetus to the Sunday-school movement, but none chose to use Sunday schools as background material to any of their other novels.

Mrs Gaskell (1810–65), the early biographer of Charlotte Brontë, has Evangelical understanding but shows little interest in Sunday schools in her writing. In *Ruth* (1853) Ruth Dillon, alias Mrs Denbigh, is being sheltered as a supposedly pregnant widow by a dissenting minister Mr Benson and his sisters. We are given an account of what happened in the house on Sunday. It

> was a festival and a holiday in the house. After the very early breakfast little feet pattered into Mr Benson's study, for he had a class for boys – a sort of domestic Sunday school, only that there was more talking between teachers and pupils, than dry, absolute lessons going on. Miss Benson too, had her little, neat, tippeted maidens sitting with her in the parlour; and she was far more particular in keeping them to their reading and spelling than her brother with the boys. Sally too, put in her word of instruction from the kitchen, helping, as she fancied, though her assistance was often rather *malapropos*; for instance she called out to a little fat, stupid, roly-poly girl to whom Miss Benson was busy explaining the meaning of the word quadruped –
>
> 'Quadruped, a thing wi' four legs, Jenny; a chair is a quadruped, child.'[33]

One is reminded of Mr Gradgrind's slick definitions in Dickens's *Hard Times* (1854) but neither in that novel nor in any other of his novels is there a specific reference to Sunday schools.[34] Norris Pope in a recent book has carefully recorded the extent to which Dickens was involved in the Ragged School movement. Although the RSU was not founded until 1844 Ragged Schools were not a new idea and had their origins in Ragged Sunday schools (or 'fragment schools' as they were sometimes called after our Lord's command to his disciples to 'gather up the fragments that remain that nothing be lost') some of which began in the eighteenth century.[35] The Field Lane School in the East End of London was set in the area of the haunts of Oliver Twist whose story (1837–39) fired the imagination of would-be benefactors and received the benefit of Dickens's powerful propaganda in the novel and elsewhere. However, Dickens was a believer in schools of industry as a reforming influence rather than in the Evangelical zeal of the Sunday-school approach.

In describing a Ragged School in *Our Mutual Friend* (1864–65) Dickens is harshly critical of the Sunday activities of the school. On Sunday evenings:

> . . . an inclined plane of unfortunate infants would be handed over to the prosiest and worst of all teachers with good intentions, whom nobody would endure. Who . . . drawling on to My Dearerr Childerrenen, let us say, for example, about the beautiful coming to the Sepulchre: and repeating the word Sepulchre (commonly

used among infants) five hundred times, and never once hinting what it meant; . . . the whole hot-bed of flushed and exhausted infants exchanging measles, rashes, whooping-cough, fever, and stomach disorder, as if they were assembled in High Market for the purpose.[36]

The point is being made in his own inimitable style that Sunday schools could not be effective without better conditions and better teaching – and officials of the SSU, for example, were themselves critical of much of the instruction given at the time.[37] However, Dickens was not, on the available evidence, a supporter of Sunday schools.

George Eliot (Marian Evans) makes only passing reference to the Sunday-school movement. She first adopted as a child and then rejected as a young woman Evangelical views, but by about the mid 1830s she was forming a balanced view and still had admiration for some of the values; in any case she was steeped in a knowledge of the manse and the rectory which form the main settings for her novels. When she writes about children's religious education it is mainly in the context of revivalist preaching: in *Adam Bede* (1859) Adam learns from Dinah Morris that she first thought of preaching from the time when she was 16 (in 1790) and 'used . . . to talk to the little children and teach them'; and there is a touching scene late in the novel where she is preaching on the Common to non-church-goers, recalled by Seth Bede:

'there was one stout curly headed fellow about three or four year old, that I never saw there before. He was as naughty as could be at the beginning while I was praying, and while we was singing, but when we all sat down and Dinah began to speak, th' young un stood stock-still all at once, and began to look at her with 's mouth open, and presently he ran away from's mother and went up to Dinah, and pulled at her, like a little dog, for her to take notice of him. So Dinah lifted him up and held th' lad on her lap, while she went on speaking; and he was as good as could be till he went t' sleep – and the mother cried to see him.'[38]

In the third of the *Scenes From Clerical Life* (1858) 'Janet's Repentance', set in the late 1820s, George Eliot wrote with mixed views about children in the Sunday school influenced by a revival: They 'had their memories crammed with phrases about the blood cleansing, imputed righteousness and justification by faith alone, which an experience lying principally in chuck-farthing, hop-scotch, parental slapping and longing after unattainable lollypops served rather to darken than to illustrate.'[39]

When Marian Evans was in a London publishing house she worked beside William Hale White (1831–1913) and they encouraged each other in their writing. Hale White, who later became a civil servant and wrote under the name of 'Mark Rutherford', spent his early years in Bedford under the influence of the 'Bunyan Meeting'. Eventually he rebelled against the Calvinism and fundamentalism of their doctrines and was expelled (unfairly) from New College, Cheshunt, where he was training for the Congregational ministry. His writings are a 'moving mixture of autobiography and fiction' in which he sensitively records the development and outcome of his 'deliverance'. Some argue that 'his books are not novels at all in any accepted sense, but tracts, sketches, conversation pieces; or that, as novels, they are in construction amateurish',[40] but Matthew Arnold was enthusiastic about them and D. H. Lawrence found them thorough, sound, and beautiful.

But again his references to Sunday schools are very scant. In *The Autobiography of Mark Rutherford* (1889) he describes how after the family prayers and breakfast 'the business of the day began with Sunday-school at nine o'clock. We were taught the Catechism and the Bible there till a quarter past ten. We were then marched across the road into the chapel.'[41] There is nothing exceptional about this at all. In *The Revolution in Tanners Lane* (1887) we find the minister's son, Thomas Brood, who 'was a teacher in the Sunday School' falling into disgrace, and a strong description of 'Brother Scotton' who 'was a Cowfold man, tall and thin, superintendent of the Sunday school and to a considerable extent independent of village custom. He was also an auctioneer, and a land surveyor; he also valued furniture and when there were any houses to be let, drew up agreements, made inventories and had even been known to prepare leases. There was always therefore a legal flavour about him.'[42] We do not know how his character expressed itself in the schoolroom.

Mrs Tonna as 'Charlotte Elizabeth' (1821–99), a leading Evangelical novelist, builds up a fair picture of the influence of Sunday schools in *Helen Fleetwood* (1841). The theme of this novel is the social and religious condition of factory work contrasted with the idyllic life of the countryside. Helen, an adopted child, thought her Sunday-school class in her village gave 'perfect satisfaction'. The widowed family was inveigled out of the village to the industrial north to prevent them from being a charge on the poor rate. They determined to keep up their Christian profession so Mrs Green looked for a Sunday school for the children.

> The Sunday school was opened long before they could arrive from the late breakfast table, with their dilatory conductor; and a very cursory view of it determined the widow not to enter her children there. Such an uninteresting, heavy-looking set of scholars she had never seen; nor was their personal appearance as to cleanliness such as to invite a near approach. The greater numbers were dozing over their tasks and the principal business of the teacher seemed to be that of shaking or cuffing them out of their lethargy, into which they presently relapsed, and Mrs Green seeing that her own children were disposed to laugh at the odd appearance of the little slumberers, soon withdrew, intending to walk in the church-yard until the hour of service.[43]

By the next Sunday a more suitable school had been found. Supposedly the references are drawn into the story to show the Christian background of the children, which would be sorely tried in the factory environment.

The scant references of Mrs Tonna to Sunday schools are, as we have seen, fuller than those by many of the major or minor novelists of the nineteenth century. Important works may have been missed but the trend is obvious: Sunday schools do not appear to make appealing reading and this is surprising considering the sympathetic support which the general public gave to them. Perhaps they were not considered a suitable area for the consideration of human conflict and maybe children were 'to be seen and not heard' in fiction as well as in life. The class issue may be another reason. Sunday schools may not have been within the experience of many readers. In Maria Charlesworth's novel *Ministering Children* (1854) Rose who comes from a 'superior' household returns home from a boarding school and wishes to attend the local Sunday school; she is afraid that her mother will not let her attend. Miss Clifford, the teacher, finds a way out: 'If you could tell me why you wished to perhaps I could find some other way to help you if your mother objects to your coming to Sunday school' and indeed a special time of instruction was set aside for Ruth and her friends of equal social standing.[44]

When we examine children's literature about Sunday schools

the picture is completely different: from Hannah More, who starts writing in the eighteenth century, through the following century there is a wealth of literary material which throws light on the way the Sunday school operates. Hannah More (1745–1833) in *Tom White the Post Boy, Mick Giles the Poacher, The History of Hester Wilmot* and above all *The Sunday School*[45] has many references to detailed ways in which Sunday schools function. Lucy Lyttleton Cameron, sister of Mrs Sherwood, has a tract called *The Sunday School Teachers* which demonstrates how children of ten years of age were Sunday-school teachers and how their diligence was rewarded by gifts to themselves and their impoverished but faithful parents.[46] Mrs Cameron merits a monograph to herself as her writing for children is prolific. John Ashworth in *Strange Tales for Humble Folk* (1865) and *Simple Records* (1871) has a large number of short stories about Sunday-school life and his topics are those taken up by the adult novelists we have analysed. The language of writers such as these is plain and at time limited but they deserve much fuller treatment in that their work constitutes an important contribution to the nineteenth-century literature on Sunday schools.

The Sunday-school movement has produced some writing which is banal and cliché-ridden. The year 1880 had its fair share of inane offerings. A musical called 'Robert Raikes, the man of Gloucester' includes these verses:

> To the good man of Gloucester
> We raise a cheerful strain,
> His heart was mov'd with sorrow
> To see sin's iron reign.
> Old age corrupt and heavy
> Defied his ardent powers;
> Said he 'We'll try another way
> The children shall be ours.'
>
> The class met, the hymns were sung,
> The class it had no teacher;
> T'was like a church with people full,
> The pulpit, with no preacher.
> Then in the timeless teacher came,
> His voice was sharp and surly
> Said he 'You know I'm not to blame
> They begin the school too early.'

The conclusion is almost sacrilegious in its crudity: 'Let us pray Lord, make me a drop of ink to write Thy Name!'[47] Such so-called literary efforts are intended to advertise the movement and tell us nothing about what really happened in Sunday schools. It is hoped that the extracts given in this paper are more illuminating and that there are more examples of 'fictional truth' which will add to our knowledge of an important and neglected aspect of English social, religious and educational life in the nineteenth century. Sunday schools have been as much neglected by the historians[48] as they appear to have been by the novelists.

NOTES

1 Unfortunately some of the Minutes and Reports of the Sunday School Union (founded in 1803) were destroyed in the blitz during the Second World War, there are no manuscript records of the Sunday School Society (founded in 1875), although eventually its limited funds were taken over by the SSU, and there is the same deficiency in the records of the Sunday School Institute (founded in 1843). Nevertheless, in spite of the gaps the available knowledge is enormous.

2 C. R. Newby, *The Story of Sunday Schools* (1936), p. 27.

3 Gloucester 13 December 1785, Ely Diocesan Records 13 6/1/9.

4 Arnold Bennett, *Clayhanger* (1910), 15th edn, September 1947.

5 Robert L. Wolff, *Gains and Losses, Novels of Faith and Doubt in Victorian England* (1977), pp. 1–2.

6 W. A. Craik, *Elizabeth Gaskell and the English Provincial Novel* (1970), p. 214.

7 Margaret O. W. Oliphant, *Salem Chapel* (1863), pp. 24 and 78–9.

8 Gerald J. Clifford, 'History as Experiences: The use of Personal-History Documents in the History of Education', *History of Education*, 1.3, p. 186.

9 The publication of the journal *Literature and History*, now in its fifth year, is one example of this new interest. In sociology the phenomenological perspective which stresses the way individuals define their own situation has been in vogue but is to some extent on the wane now (see A. Hargreaves 'Synthesis and the study of strategies: a project for the sociological imagination' (1979) in P. Woods (ed.), *Pupil Strategies* (forthcoming)).

10 P. Widdowson, P. Stigant, and P. Booker, 'History and Literary Value: The case of *Adam Bede* and *Salem Chapel*', *Literature and History* 5:1, Spring 1979.

11 R. Johnson, 'Notes on the schooling of the English working class 1780–1850' in R. Dale *et al.* (eds) *Schooling and Capitalism, a sociological reader*, (1976), pp. 44–54.

12 A. Chedzoy, 'Fictional Truth: literary education as an account of reality'

(1978), *Oxford Journal of Education* 4:3, p. 268, quoting from Sir Philip Sidney, *An Apology for Poetry* (1595).

13 Charles Shaw, *When I was a Child* (1977). This book originally appeared as a series of anonymous articles in the *Staffordshire Sentinel* from December 1892 to May 1893 and was first published in 1903 under the anonym 'An Old Potter'.

14 See R. Currie, *Methodism Divided, A Study in the Sociology of Ecumenicalism* (1968).

15 (*a*) *Methodist Magazine*, November 1831; (*b*) Minutes of the Methodist New Connexion, e.g. 1826, 1836, 1895; (*c*) A private communication with Robert Currie shows that the number of scholars reached its peak in 1906 at 88,522 but there had been a falling away between 1890 and 1905.

16 H. Goldstraw, 'The Rise and Development of Education in the Staffordshire Potteries' (1955, unpublished M.Ed. thesis).

17 Sunday School Union, Reports of Deputations, 1946, pp. 241–2.

18 Charles Shaw, op. cit., pp. 6–8.

19 Arnold Bennett, op. cit., p. 125.

20 Ibid., p. 28.

21 Ibid., p. 31.

22 Ibid., pp. 248 and 252.

23 The *raw* numbers of children attending Sunday school (independent of the percentage of the age group) began to decline in the early years of the twentieth century. For example the 2,433,000 Church of England scholars in 1911 had declined to 1,994,000 by 1921 and in the United Methodist Church the decline in attendance began almost as soon as it was established from 315,993 in 1908 to 262,595 in 1921. (See Minutes of the UMC and *Facts and Figures about the Church of England*.)

24 Gillian Avery, *Childhood's Pattern – A study of the heroes and heroines of children's fiction 1770–1950* (1965), p. 72.

25 77th Report of the SSU 1878–79 and 78th Report 1879–80.

26 Arnold Bennett, op. cit., pp. 227–8.

27 Arnold, Bennett, op. cit., pp. 236–7 and 241–2.

28 Arnold Bennett, *Anna of the Five Towns* (1900). Penguin edn, 1967, pp. 15 ff.; 31–2; 54–5, 58, 230; and 127–43. The background has been carefully researched with reference to the Primitive Methodist recession in Burslem in 1808, the Warren Affair of 1828, and the 1849 Fly Sheets.

29 Ibid., pp. 127–43.

30 Charlotte Brontë, *Shirley* (1844; Everyman edn, 1955), pp. 229–30.

31 *The Times*, 27 June 1880.

32 Charlotte Brontë, op. cit., pp. 240–41.

33 Elizabeth Gaskell, *Ruth* (1853), p. 65.

34 Private communication with Prof. P. Collins, author of *Dickens and Education*.

35   In 1817 'The Fragment Sunday School' was opened in Maid Lane, Bankside, Southwark, under the control of Surrey Chapel. Other such schools were opened in the City including one in Lambeth (1838). 'These schools were early visited by Lord Ashley and other distinguished noblemen and M.P.s., who, seeing their benefits, began to exert their influence in encouraging the formation of similar schools throughout the metropolis', *Primitive Methodist Magazine* (May 1951), p. 281).

36   Quoted by Morris Pope, *Dickens and Charity* (1978), p. 197. His chapter on the Ragged School Movement (pp. 152–99) is drawn upon heavily here.

37   The SSU Deputations have already been noted. Various publications of the SSU, e.g. H. Althans, *The Scripture Teacher Assistant* (1833) and L. Davids (1847) seek to give positive help to teachers.

38   George Eliot, *Adam Bede* (1859), pp. 75 and 434–6.

39   Quoted by Robert L. Wolff, *Gains and Losses,Novels of Faith and Doubt in Victorian England* (1977), pp. 234–5.

40   William Hale White (Mark Rutherford), *The Revolution in Tanner's Lane* (1887; 1971 edn, Introduction by Simon Nowell Smith), p. vii.

41   William Hale White *The Autobiography of Mark Rutherford and Mark Rutherford's Deliverance edited by his friend, Reuben Sharp* (1889), pp. 5–6.

42   William Hale White, *The Revolution in Tanner's Lane*, p. 326.

43   'Charlotte Elizabeth', *Mrs Fleetwood* (1841), p. 80.

44   Maria Charlesworth, *Ministering Children* (1854), pp. 41–2.

45   Hannah More, *Works* (1830), vols iv and vii.

46   Lucy L. Cameron, *The Sunday School Teachers* (1830), no. 6 of Houlston's Series of Tracts.

47   E. P. Hood, *Robert Raikes the man of Gloucester, A musical Memoir* (1880).

48   Thomas W. Laqueur, *Religion and Respectability: Sunday Schools and Working Class Culture 1780–1850* (1976) has made a useful contribution, but the study is limited chronologically and geographically, and his thesis that Sunday schools became truly working-class establishments is suspect and needs further investigation.

Two Centuries
and Six Continents After

Gerald E. Knoff

One of the catchwords in American Christian education circles in the 1960s was 'If it doesn't happen in the local church it doesn't happen'. The warning was in part an emphasis upon the need for parish vitality, in part a disillusionment with national programmes. As is the case with most slogans, it had truth in it; truth, and fallacy as well.

The growth of the world Sunday-school movement was one instance of a local venture spreading and growing far beyond its local confines, finally to be known and felt in most of the Christian world.

Robert Raikes, called of God, rose to meet a Gloucester problem. He lived to see the modest venture he established there spread to most of England. Whether he had an intimation that the Sunday school would in time reach other countries, and across several oceans, I do not know.

A hundred years later, however, that is exactly what happened, and the Sunday-school movement could without exaggeration be said to be worldwide. This essay attempts in brief compass to recount that amazing spread.

The Phenomenal Growth of the
Early Sunday-school Movement

Many of the early accounts of the spread of the Sunday schools are filled with such exuberance that one is inclined to wonder at the accuracy of the reporting. Yet there seems ample evidence that the Sunday schools, often modelled upon those begun by Robert Raikes and his associates, rapidly were accepted for many reasons and spread quickly throughout the United Kingdom. Three reasons have been advanced for this expansion by Thomas Laqueur. The Sunday schools were seen as an instrument for the moral rescue of poor children from corrupt parents; they were an effective means for spreading the Word of God; and a new, soft, kind, and more opti-

mistic view of children had begun to be felt coming from philosophers such as Locke and Rousseau and poets such as Wordsworth
and Blake.[1]

In addition to these factors it should be pointed out that the
Sunday schools were a part of the immense vitality of middle and
late nineteenth-century British voluntary societies.

> As the hearse containing the Earl of Shaftesbury's coffin made its
> way to Westminster Abbey on October 8, 1885, it passed through
> streets lined with deputations from ragged schools, costermongers'
> and flower girls' relief societies, missions, refuges, and training
> ships. Many of them held banners on which they had painstak-
> ingly woven such texts as 'I was naked and ye clothed me' and 'I
> was a stranger and ye took me in'.[2]

As early as 1810, a year before Raikes's death, it was reported that
in Britain there were more than three thousand Sunday schools
established and nearly 275,000 'scholars educated'.[3]

The story of the influence of Robert Raikes in Britain is, however,
dealt with at greater length by other contributors to this volume.
The growth of the movement in the United States may be less
familiar to British readers.

The Sunday school was an import, but an import which quickly
became an accepted part of the American religious scene.

As was the case in the mother country, the aims were both
religious and secular.

> Usually organized groups of benevolent citizens formed schools,
> first in eastern seaboard cities, with two predominant aims. They
> wanted to bring the children and young people to Christ, and they
> wanted to train them in the three 'R's' and Christian morality so
> that they would be safe and useful citizens.[4]

The origin was openly admitted by one of the chroniclers: 'Robert
Raikes laid the corner-stone of an edifice, unsurpassed as yet, in the
simple majesty of its structure, and the enduring usefulness of its
destination.'[5]

There was one factor which tremendously accelerated the growth
of the Sunday-school movement in early nineteenth-century United
States, the opening up of the Mississippi valley and the Great Plains
to emigrants from the Atlantic seaboard, leading in time to the
creation of political territories which later became admitted States of

the Union. Baptist, Methodist, and Presbyterian missionaries were often the intrepid heralds of the gospel, and as their weary horses turned away from an Ohio forest settlement, a little Sabbath or Sunday school was left behind to represent the Church of Christ until the arrival of the next itinerant evangelist.

And these Sunday schools grew as the people came from over the Appalachians in ever-increasing numbers. Often organizationally independent of the churches, the Sunday schools in time reached out and clasped hands with one another to form Sunday school unions in towns, counties, states, finally to form the International Sunday School Association. This was a somewhat pretentious name for an agency embracing Sunday schools in the United States and Canada.

By the close of the century it could be reported for one State that every county was organized for Sunday-school work and was holding a convention to inspire its workers. One million, six hundred thousand persons were involved, one-fourth the population of the State.[6]

No matter if most of these Pennsylvania workers had only the foggiest notion of who Robert Raikes was, and when and where he lived. They were still his spiritual descendants.

The Effects of the Movement Intended and Otherwise

One of the reasons for the promotion of the Sunday schools in the early nineteenth century was the advancement of literacy, strange as that may seem to us in these days of State-supported education. In the United States, particularly in the newer territories and States, the Sunday school provided a stand-in for elementary education, fulfilling this role until the public schools were established and able to care for the need.[7] The Sunday schools in many areas so prepared the way for the later common schools of the villages and towns.[8]

In Britain the same motivations were present conspicuously in the very first schools in Gloucester, and operated well into the century. In a booklet, *Plan of a Society . . . for the Support and Encouragement of Sunday Schools*, published in 1810, the first object named is that, 'poor persons of each sex, of any age, . . . shall be taught to read. . . .' Those who could acquire such a skill elsewhere were to do so, the Sunday schools being intended for the needy.[9]

This restriction gives a hint of another effect of the Sunday schools: they were instruments of a class society, a characteristic more conspicuous in Britain than in the United States and Canada. According to the 'Rules' mentioned above, children admitted to the Sunday school were to be those who by poverty were deprived of learning on the weekdays.

As delegates assembled for the first World Convention in London in 1889 there were reports indicating that Sunday schools in Europe, Britain, Australia, and to a lesser extent in the United States were thought of as being operated for the poor and lower classes, the upper classes being largely untouched by these schools.[10] In the United States a singular blindness related to slavery persisted, and the leaders of the Sunday-school movement had little or nothing to say about this institution, a silence which was all too often found in the churches themselves, in the North as well as in the South.[11]

The efforts towards literacy and the acceptance of a socially structured society were part of a broader influence of the Sunday schools: their role as preparation for middle-class respectability. There was surely room for that role in late eighteenth-century Gloucester, and Robert Raikes was confident his efforts had helped juvenile behaviour.

> In those parishes where the plan has been adopted, we are assured that the behaviour of the children is greatly civilized. The barbarous ignorance in which they had before lived being in some degree dispelled, they begin to give proofs that those persons are mistaken who consider the lower orders of mankind incapable of improvement and therefore think an attempt to reclaim them impracticable, or, at least, not worth the trouble.[12]

Motivated by many considerations, not the least of which was the spiritual improvement of the young, the Sunday schools developed into a widespread religious movement, first in all three English-speaking nations, then into most of the Protestant world. They were often, indeed usually, led by laymen, and in Britain mostly of Dissenter origin, the Church of England being slow to see much good in the innovations.

In America, as well, the Sunday schools were often independent or quasi-independent institutions, and only gradually did they 'join the church': 'In one sense the long story of the American Sunday school could be interpreted as the progressive baptism of the Sunday school into ecclesiastical respectability. The practice was rarely smooth, and the result never fully achieved.'[13]

The Sunday-school movement was not without its detractors and opponents. In Britain the opposition sometimes (often rightly) charged that they reflected their Dissenter origins and therefore were not to be trusted by sound Anglicans. Sometimes the Sunday schools were accused of being part of a Jacobite plot, even though Culloden Moor was more than fifty years in the past.

By 1803 the Sunday School Union was formed and by the end of the century denominations had begun to awaken to their own, official responsibility.[14]

The Sunday schools in America also found an unofficial inter-denominational structure the most useful sponsorship for their work. The Philadelphia First Day Society was one of the first, and the crying needs in the sparsely settled Mississippi valley made the efforts of such agencies as the American Sunday School Union with its missionaries virtually indispensable.

In time, as the population increased and the cities began to grow, most of them situated along the great rivers of the Ohio and the Mississippi, and beside the two Great Lakes, Erie and Michigan, local Sunday School Unions began to form themselves into larger units. They established county and State Sunday school unions, not always in that order. In time delegates from these bodies formed a State society, and later delegates from the State unions formed the International Sunday School Association.[15] Pyramidal structures were thus established with each base formed of smaller geographical entities.

The Early International Beginnings

It would be natural to suppose that there would exist a considerable fraternity between the (British) Sunday School Union and the International Sunday School Association. This, indeed, was the case.

In 1886 the Executive Committee of the latter body met at Lake Chautauqua, New York, and during its sessions, B. F. Jacobs, one of its most active lay leaders, urged that a World Convention be called and held in London. The next year the full Convention approved the idea and the call was issued, with the co-operation of

Edward Towers, one of the honorary secretaries of the London Sunday School Union. So it was that the first World Sunday School Convention was held in London, 1–6 July 1889.

In successive years these Conventions were held, often at three- or four-year intervals. London was the host city for two of them, as was Tokyo. Three were held in the U.S.A. (St. Louis, Washington, and Los Angeles); three in continental Europe (Rome, Zurich, and Oslo); one each in Jerusalem, Glasgow, Rio de Janeiro, and Toronto. The last Convention was that in Tokyo, 1958, when it was decided that the time, expense, and effort in planning, promoting, and holding such mass gatherings might better be expended in other directions.

The Americans who attended the overseas conventions in the early years lost no time aboard the ship in organizing lecture series, conferences on Sunday school work, corporate worship, and actual Sunday schools with teachers and officers drawn from the seafaring delegates. What we would call boosterism, akin to collegiate athletics, was conspicuous.

> Hi-O-hi, O-hi-o,
> We make music where we go!
> Never sulk, never sour,
> Jerusalem, Jerusalem, Nineteen Four. OHIO.[16]

This was the group yell of delegates from a State which does not have to be further identified.

At the next convention (Washington, 1910) a song from the Illinois delegation was more sombre, since some of the great leaders of the movement, and indeed of American evangelical Protestanism, had recently died.

> Not without thy wondrous glory,
> Illinois, Illinois,
> Can be writ the nation's story,
> Illinois, Illinois,
> On the record of thy years,
> Dwight L. Moody's name appears,
> Jacobs, Reynolds and our tears, Illinois, Illinois.[17]

There were more to these voyages, however, than hoop-la, for the pilgrims were responsive to the missionary and evangelistic impulses of the gospel. Evangelistic services were held on board ship for the passengers and the crew alike. Conversions were expected and experienced. On one ship *en route* to the fifth convention in Rome, 1907, seventeen thousand dollars was raised for missionary and world Sunday-school work. In addition as a result of stops in North Africa, nearly fifty thousand dollars was raised for Methodist missions in Algeria.[18]

The World's Sunday School Association in its Early Years

Arrangements for these early conventions were in the hands of either the British or the American body, depending upon the location of the gathering and interim structures were minimal. In time these provisions proved inadequate, the work-load being too heavy for the already burdened secretaries in London and Chicago.

As a result, at the Rome Convention in 1907 a formal organization was established with an appropriate constitution and by-laws and with the name *World's Sunday School Association*, changing in time to the *World Council of Christian Education*.

These early conventions and the early years of the WSSA were characterized by a buoyant optimism that the future held for the movement only glorious hopes and uninterrupted progress toward a kingdom of light and joy. This roseate expectation was the motivating force which led preachers, lay people, and whole congregations to labour zealously for their Lord and for the coming of his Kingdom, a Kingdom and a Second Advent which surely could not be far in the future.

Proof? Well, not quite proof, but look what the Lord had done in Lancashire, in Wisconsin, look to the newly established and flourishing work in India, and see, in places such as these, harbingers of the day when every knee would bow to the victorious Christ. And in the preparing of the way, the Sunday school was obviously playing a significant role.

The conventions are to be seen not really as educational assemblies as we would use the term today but as great mass meetings, suffused with an intense missionary and evangelistic spirit. They were part of the revival and evangelistic movements of the late nineteenth century. They shared in the vigorous missionary efforts of the same period, programmes emanating for the most part from Berlin, London, and New York.

Were these Sunday-school efforts paternalistic in spirit and origin? They certainly were. The WSSA began its life dominated by leaders in Britain and the United States. It continued long in that direction and only with great difficulty was responsibility truly shared with representatives of the younger churches.

> Shall we whose lamps are lighted
> With wisdom from on high,
> Shall we to souls benighted
> The lamp of life deny?

The words of Reginald Heber were well known to these convention goers and they found in them no trace of the supercilious.

This paternalism had another aspect, an intense and unquestioned domination of the conventions and the whole movement by those from the United States and Britain. In these gatherings which proudly called themselves world conventions, 'God Save the King' and 'America' were frequently sung, the identical music making one seem only a following stanza of the first. In all of the fourteen conventions there is a record of only one other national anthem being sung.[19] Singers from other nations seemingly were expected to be musically mute.

Interest in the social issues of the world emerged only slowly. In the first conventions the traditional pietistic concerns were frequently expressed; the use of beverage alcohol, Sabbath or Sunday observance, 'piety and personal purity in the home'.

Concern for the evils of industrialism, urbanization, colonialism, for world peace, for the welfare of workers emerged after a time in the later conventions. Margaret Slattery of Boston and Joseph Parker of London's City Temple were especially articulate.

In the late 1930s there occurred a complication which might have tested the commitment of the Association to complete racial equality. A convention was planned for 1940 in Durban. Assurances were made that all delegates would be received in a satisfactory manner, but it appeared before long that some kind of segregated pattern would be encountered. In spite of the efforts of the American General Secretary, Robert M. Hopkins, the matter was never fully resolved, and before long the outbreak of World War II made the controversy irrelevant.

The Association (*Council*) Becomes
a Professional Body

The reason the two names are used in the heading is that the World's Sunday School Association changed its name to World Council of Christian Education, then to World Council of Christian Education and Sunday School Association, and finally back to World Council of Christian Education. There were valid organizational reasons for the changes in nomenclature, but they lie beyond the scope of this brief review.

It would be incorrect to say that the WSSA was a lay organization, for there were ministers who were leaders, both in its conventions and in the continuing work of the body. It did, however, have a lay tradition and one which was symbolized in the series of its Presidents, laymen who presided over most of its later years.

Of these lay Presidents, Sir Harold (later Lord and still later Viscount) Mackintosh was easily the most influential. He was named President at the Los Angeles convention in 1928. He continued in this office for thirty years, when he became the Chairman of the Council, a position which he held until his death the day after Christmas, 1964 – thirty-six years of continuous service and leadership.

While Sir Harold was a layman there was elected as Chairman at the same convention, Dr Luther A. Weigle of New Haven, Connecticut. He had been the Horace Bushnell Professor of Christian Nurture at Yale University and soon came to be the dominant educational figure in the WSSA. He was named Dean of Yale's Divinity School the same year of the Los Angeles Convention.

The two men, the British Methodist layman and the American Congregational minister formed an unusual pair, and a warm personal friendship matured between them which lasted until Viscount Mackintosh's death.

The position of Chairman was in reality more influential in the basic programme of the Association than that of President and by the time of the Rio de Janeiro convention in 1932 and the Oslo convention in 1936 Weigle's influence in the direction of a sound and forceful educational programme was being felt.

Another influence towards the professionalization of the organization came in 1939 when Dr Forrest L. Knapp became the American General Secretary of the body. He was the first executive in the life of the agency who was professionally trained as a religious educator. A former student of Dr Weigle, and with a background of work in a city and in a national educational council, Knapp brought a useful professional experience to the agency it had not before possessed.

No material exists upon which an analysis of those attending the several conventions from 1928 onwards could be constructed. But it is probable that there was a larger number of persons with some amount of professional educational training attending these meetings than was previously the case.

One of the chief concerns of Dr Knapp was the divided administrative responsibility of the Association. Growing out of its origins as the creature of an American and a British body, the Association had two equal programme groups, two equal General Secretaries, and not until the annual meeting of the Board of Managers (it had earlier names) or the Quadrennial meeting of the Assembly was any official unity manifest.

There were those on both sides of the Atlantic who saw in this division strength instead of weakness, and valued the more intimate relationships made possible thus with member units around the world.

In time, however, sentiment swung sharply to an awareness of the weaknesses and the anomalies of this bifurcated structure, and at the Toronto convention meetings in 1950 it was decided to unify the structure and programme.

To that end a new office of a single General Secretary was created and to it was called Nelson Chappel, a Canadian. He had been the executive of the Religious Education Council of Canada, like Knapp a professional educator.

Dr Knapp had vigorously championed this development, realizing that his advocacy made him an unlikely selection for this new position even should his professional desires for the organization be supported. Accordingly when Chappel assumed the newly created top administrative post, Dr Knapp resigned his New York position and accepted other work.

Dr Chappel soon discovered that it was easier to vote for the legislation than it was to effect the desired organizational changes. The British committee zealously guarded its funds, the Americans did the same, and a truly unified budget never really came about. And without a unified budget the organization failed often to act as a unified whole.

Because of failing eyesight Chappel elected early retirement, but before he left he insisted that the governing bodies of the WCCESSA, as it was then called, face up to its inadequacies, and make a reality of the directives which had been imperfectly observed since the Toronto Assembly fifteen years before.

The new General Secretary, Ralph N. Mould, an American United Presbyterian minister, had been familiar with the programme of the Council from its Toronto convention. At the Belfast Assembly (1962) he was one of those who cogently urged closer relationships with the World Council of Churches. He was now called upon to expedite as chief executive what he had urged as a voting member of its governing body.

But first there must be achieved the delicate task of unifying the programme and work of the fractured Council. His directions from his policy-makers were explicit enough:

> Set yourself up in Geneva, improve relationships with the World Council of Churches, make of the World Council of Christian Education and Sunday School Association a single body, and see to it that New York and London support you in that grand design.

Evolving Relationships with the World Council of Churches

The directive given to Ralph Mould marked a new development in the life of the World Council of Christian Education and Sunday School Association, a serious pursuit of relationships with the World Council of Churches.

The founding of the World Council of Churches in Amsterdam in 1948 was accompanied by the realization in both Councils that the churches' work in Christian Education was a matter of concern to both, and that relationships would have to be carefully worked out. The World Council of Churches from its very beginning under the direction of a Provisional Committee had many programmes which were educational in nature and scope, educational in everything but the name.

One of its most vigorous units was its Youth Department, and because of this programme the WCCESSA became most directly involved in WCC affairs. Sometimes the involvement was mutually beneficial, sometimes it was something short of harmonious.

A serious complication was that youth work had been established first by the American section of the WCCE and only later became a programme of the whole body. The British Committee, more than the American, remained vividly aware of the worthy heritage of work with children and only gradually did some of its members see the importance of work with young people.

Forrest Knapp, on the other hand, and most of the American leaders were keenly aware not only of the intrinsic value of youth programmes, but saw plainly that to allow this important aspect of the churches' work to be pre-empted entirely by the World Council of Churches would be a failure of resolve.

Accordingly over the years various types of committee relationships were adopted, modified, and discarded. Tensions developed from time to time, sometimes between the two agencies, sometimes within the WCCESSA itself, caused by different educational viewpoints, sometimes by lack of internal clearances with the office of the General Secretary.

On the whole, however, effective co-operation increased. The establishment of a Geneva office of the WCCESSA in 1963 assisted greatly in common understandings as the deeply respected Herbert A. Hamilton came to the Ecumenical Centre in that city. The arrival of Donald O. Newby, an American youth leader, from a post in Africa furthered the common effort. Before long work with and for young people in Geneva was functionally one work.

Meanwhile representatives of the WCC attended Assemblies of the WCCESSA and persons from the WCCESSA sat as consultants or fraternal delegates in meetings of the WCC Assemblies and Central Committee in the 1950s and thereafter.

A World Convention of Christian Education in Tokyo in 1958 and a World Christian Youth Conference in Kottayam, India, in 1952 afforded opportunities for effective collaboration between the youth staffs and supporting bodies of the two agencies.

The co-operation between the two youth departments, while it was not always complete, indeed sometimes stormy, was on the whole effective. In a real sense it was the precursor of the union of the two Councils. Perhaps it is not too much to say that, had not this co-operation of youth leaders grown in common understanding and respect, the two Councils would have required another ten years to arrive at the ultimate actions taken in Addis Ababa, Ethiopia, and Huampani, Peru, in 1971.

The Merger of the Two World Bodies

While inconclusive and unofficial conversations had taken place between representatives of the WCC and the WCCESSA in the 1950s, it was during the year 1961 that serious consideration of the problems and possibilities involved really began in earnest.

In that year the WCC came to the conclusion that it was necessary for it to establish an official unit on education. It was looking forward to a complete merger with the International Missionary Council at its New Delhi Assembly scheduled for November 1961. This decision was not made by itself alone, for full clearances were made with the executive of the WCCESSA, Nelson Chappel.

The General Assembly of the WCC decided to establish such an office with an emphasis first upon general education and its relation to the work of the churches, but with other emphases to be developed later.

There was little feeling in the WCCESSA that this action infringed its prerogatives. Just the opposite. It was accepted by most as an assumption of an unavoidable responsibility of the WCC and one which made possible creative new approaches between the two bodies.

In that spirit a decisive action was taken at the Belfast Assembly of the WCCESSA (1962) affirming

> . . . our desire to explore and improve our procedures for co-operation with and our relationship to the World Council of Churches without prejudice or commitment as to specific measures for the future – and asking the staff to prepare a statement on existing relationships, co-operative activities, and possibly overlapping activities, and on the purpose, structure and work of both the WCC and the WCCESSA, indicating similarities and differences in the matters and this would involve full and frank discussion between the staff members of the two organizations. The Board also asked the Secretaries to prepare a statement setting out the composition of our member units and their relationship to the churches and to other ecumenical bodies.[20]

Accompanying this action there was a position statement drafted and approved which displayed maximum openness for the future.

The WCCESSA is not primarily concerned about preserving its present patterns of work and structure in comparison to more effectively meeting the tremendous needs of the world to which God leads us as His servants. Nor does the WCCESSA see Christian education, though basic, as anything more than one element of total church life and work. The WCCESSA is willing in the context and under the urgency of mission to a world in crisis to modify its organizational life, in whatever degree or ways may appear necessary, in order to render a greater Christian education witness and ministry, to and through all churches, on behalf of the whole world God loves. To know Christ and to make Him known is our plumb line.[21]

Before long it was agreed by the two world bodies that the first joint venture under this new action would be the preparation of a joint statement on the nature and scope of education, both in and outside the Church. Appointments were made by both bodies and Kathleen Bliss of England, long active in the national education programme of the Church of England and Divisional Chairwoman of the WCC, was elected by the Joint Commission itself to be its presiding officer.

Meetings began in 1964 and continued, either as a committee of the whole or as sessions of an Executive Committee, until the summer of 1967. Staff assistance was given by Father Paul Verghese of the WCC and by Herbert A. Hamilton and later Ralph Mould of the WCCESSA. In time Theodore A. Gill of the U.S.A. was secured as the writer of the report and in the summer of 1968 he presented the report of the Joint Commission to the Fourth General Assembly of the WCC in Uppsala, and just before that to the meeting of the Board of Managers of the WCCE in Frankfurt.[22]

Not long after the adoption of this report the two Councils took an action proposing what had been long in their minds and what had been implicit in recently adopted actions: the consideration of a formal and complete merger of the two world organizations. The Nairobi Assembly of the WCCE took the enabling action and soon thereafter the Central Committee of the WCC in Heraklion, Crete, took similar and supportive steps. Both actions came in the summer of 1967.

Again, representatives of both world councils were appointed and the first meeting of the Joint Negotiating Committee convened in

Geneva in December of 1968, with the fourth and concluding meeting held in London in June 1970. Two leaders presided over the sometimes difficult sessions, Kathleen Bliss, heading the WCC delegation and Charles Malik, then President of the WCCE.

The work of the Joint Negotiating Committee was made more difficult than it would otherwise have been by the fact that simultaneously the WCC was undergoing a radical reorganization of its own work. For the Christian Education people the question was not therefore a simple 'Shall we unite or not?' but 'If we unite what shall be the shape and form of that with which we are uniting?'

In time the uncertainties were resolved to the satisfaction of most persons involved, and the decision was made that the work and influence of the WCCE, carrying on the more than eighty years of useful work of the WSSA – indeed the tradition of Robert Raikes of Gloucester – should be further entrusted to the Office of Education of the World Council of Churches.

The WCC's central Committee met in the opening days of 1971 in Addis Ababa, and the final Assembly of the WCCE took its action in Huampani, Peru, in August of that year. Chairman (Bishop) Mueller prayed that 'God would bless and seal what we have just decided.'

It is still a long way from Gloucester to Huampani, for the geography has not shrunk. It is two hundred years from the schools Robert Raikes started and which this symposium celebrates. Emphases changed, secondary purposes became outmoded and were superseded by others. Leaders were raised up, they died, others came to take their places. Much of the rhetoric at Huampani Robert Raikes would have found incomprehensible; from some of it he would have dissented.

Yet through the years the central conviction remained constant. The gospel, not contrived by human effort, but the gift of God, is for all persons of every age, rank, and race. The presentation of this gospel by word and example is the task of every Christian. Formal and informal teaching and learning is one of the ways to present it, and in that presentation we are fulfilling the commandment of our Lord.

From Gloucester to Geneva, and then? A little book on the meaning of history, recently written by Yale's celebrated historian, Roland H. Bainton, bears the title *Yesterday, Today, and What*

Next? It might have served as a sub-title for our symposium on Robert Raikes.

NOTES

1 Thomas Walter Laqueur, *Religion and Respectability: Sunday Schools and Working Class Culture* (New Haven, Yale University Press, 1976), p. 4.

2 Ian Bradley, *The Call to Seriousness* (New York, Macmillan, 1976), p. 133.

3 *Plan of a Society, established in London, Anno Domini 1785 for the Support and Encouragement of Sunday Schools* (London, J. D. Dewick, 1810), p. 46.

4 William Bean Kennedy, *The Shaping of Protestant Education* (New York, Association Press, 1966), p. 14.

5 Thomas S. Grimke, *Sunday Schools in the Mississippi* (Philadelphia, American Sunday School Union, 1831), p. 9.

6 H. J. Heinz, *Fifth World Convention Report* (1907), p. 8.

7 See, for example, T. S. Grimke, op. cit., p. 11.

8 The great public school advocate, Henry Barnard, and the historian, E. P. Cubberley, gave such testimonies, according to William Kennedy, op. cit., pp. 21-3.

9 Thomas Walter Laqueur, op. cit., pp. 86 and 87.

10 See my *The World Sunday School Movement* (New York, Seabury Press, 1979), pp. 18-20.

11 Robert W. Lynn and Elliott Wright, *The Big Little School* (New York, Harper and Row, 1971), pp. 37 and 38.

12 Alfred Gregory, *Robert Raikes: Journalist and Philanthropist* (New York, Anson D. F. Randolph & Co., 1877), p. 78.

13 William Kennedy, op. cit., p. 65.

14 J. Kenneth Meir, *Labour of Love* (London and Nutfield, Surrey, Methodist Youth Department and National Christian Education Council, 1971), pp. 17-19.

15 Cf. p. 94 above.

16 Charles G. Trumbull, *Pilgrimage to Jerusalem* (Philadelphia, Sunday School Times, 1905), p. 9.

17 Robert W. Lynn and Elliott Wright, op. cit., p. 76.

18 For an account of these conventions and the accompanying trans-Atlantic voyages for the North American delegates, see the Convention Reports, published for every one, except for the Jerusalem meeting. See also my *The World Sunday School Movement*.

19 The Italian. In Rome, 1907.

20 *Report of the Board of Managers to the Assembly, 1962*, pp. 7 and 8.

21 *Report of the Belfast Assembly, 1962*, Exhibit 155, p. 90.

22 The name of the agency by then had been shortened.

Part III

Present and Future

Education and Society

Krister Ottosson

> I have come that men may have life,
> and may have it in all its fullness.
>
> JOHN 10.10 (N.E.B.)

At the age of fourteen, David seemed pretty normal. He was a member of his year-group football team at school. He used to go fishing with his father and he hated going shopping with his mother and sister. He was in a group at school which those in the know regarded as the 'C' stream – he wasn't going to do brilliantly in his G.C.E. 'O' level examinations at the age of sixteen, but he would do reasonably well in his C.S.E. examinations; and it was therefore likely that he might leave school to enter some kind of clerical job which might provide him with a safe, if uneventful future. He was possibly unusual in that he was a member of the local scout group which had a remarkable capacity for discovering and developing innate talent. The group staged a gang show each year, and in this David was the clown – he always took the funny parts, and audiences were in stitches whenever he was on the stage. The sense of fun and happiness about life which he exuded on those occasions seemed to say something about him as a person: he was always teasing and always joking, and he displayed an ability to mimic which some television artists would have valued. Always full of life, he also cared deeply about other people, and was near to tears when one day he went into the children's ward of a local hospital to visit a friend who had been knocked down while riding his bicycle. His elderly grandmother lived a few streets away, and he was round there every day 'just to see that she was alright'.

One evening, seven years later, a middle-aged school-teacher was having a quiet drink in a pub when a rather bashful young man came up to him, and said 'Er, excuse me, you are Mr Stevenson, aren't you?' The teacher peered into the face of the young man seeking a feature that he could recognize. 'Yes, I am. But . . . ?' 'I'm David Johnson. You taught me at school.' The older man swallowed hard to hide his embarrassment at not recognizing someone whose fourth-form master he had once been. 'I'm sorry David, I didn't recognize you. Tell me what you've been up to since you left school.' What he could have said was 'How you've changed!' but he didn't.

The young man who stood before him was very different from the boy he once knew. David told him that he was to be married in a couple of months, and that that afternoon he and his fiancée had been along to make the final arrangements to buy the small terraced house in which they were to live. David told his former school-teacher earnestly that he had a good steady job in the clerical department of a nearby government office. He furrowed his brow as he talked of the difficulties involved in raising a mortgage, and as he mapped out the way he saw his life developing. As he took his drinks to a young lady at a table in the corner of the room, the teacher reflected that, not only were David's shoulders already hunched, but also that that sparkle and spirit which had charac-terized the boy in his schooldays had now gone from his eyes, presumably for good.

Five years on from this chance meeting in a pub there is at least the faintest possibility that David will have fathered two children, and that his life will have taken on a predictable routine which might include regular shopping expeditions, nights out 'with the lads', the occasional outing with his wife, and endless evenings watching, among other things, the television commercials, because at least these provide the shared experience necessary to make con-versation possible. As for his wife's depression – he won't find that the easiest thing to handle.

Perhaps one day the as yet untamed spirit of his children will, for a brief moment, rekindle the spark of life which once moved him. Whether the spark bursts into flame or not may largely depend upon how heavily he carries the responsibility of parenthood. In any event, if he were to be asked the question, 'Are you happy?' the answer might well be an unenthusiastic, 'Well, I think so.'

But if he were to be asked whether he was living life in all its fullness, his answer might be much more straightforward. Though perhaps it would be unkind to ask him: has he not already endured the destruction of his spirit? Is that not punishment enough, without reminding him of the dreams that he once had and of the possibilities that, as a child, conceivably lay before him?

But the question has to be asked, if not of David, at least of those who, in some way or another, influence the course of events affecting the lives of young people in the journey from adolescence to adulthood. And behind that question lie a number of other critical questions which have to be faced: Is the living of life in all its abundance and fullness remotely a possibility in this life? And if it is, then is such living the birthright of everyone, or the prerogative of a few? In the attainment of full and abundant living, how important, relative to one another, are the subjugation of innate spirits and the cultivation and stimulation of those same spirits? How do we find the necessary balance between conformity and creativity, knowing that one society's creativity is another's conformity? What roles does institutionalized education play in enabling those who experience it to live their lives fully and abundantly? When does it fulfil that liberating objective, and when does it collude with the demonic forces at work in every society domesticating and taming its free spirits?

Education, Society, and the Transmission of Values

Educationists will argue endlessly about whether educational institutions reflect social values or whether they are able to give expression to alternatives. While clearly there is a measure of chicken and egg in this, it remains true that these institutions do transmit values, many of which have the tacit approval of society generally.

The Identification of Education with Schools and Universities

While it is a fact that most people learn most of the things that are important to them outside the walls of institutions normally referred to as educational, it still remains true that when a person is asked where he received his education the questioner is really asking where he went to school and university. The importance of noticing this point lies in recognizing the social kudos which is accorded those who attain success in institutional education, and the belittling of the content of the learning received outside schools by those who do not succeed at school.

Of course everyone agrees that the home experiences of a child in the first five years of its life are the most important it will ever know. But once the child is of school age, the focus of attention of friends and relatives shifts from the child's natural developmental progress ('Isn't he learning to talk well.' 'Look how he's grown!')

to concern about his school achievement ('John's at the top table in the reception class.' 'Penny's already reached book 3 in her reading'). So, learning the things that school is trying to teach becomes more important than absorbing things that are learned elsewhere. Take the matter of holidays, for instance: schools regularly take parties of pupils on trips abroad because the educational value of such experiences is recognized. Equally, parents are permitted to keep their children away from school for a couple of weeks at the end of the summer term if they wish to take family holidays at that time. But one suspects that this is a concession on the part of schools rather than a recognition of the educational value of family holidays – even continental family holidays. And if parents wish to keep their children away from school for a longer period than a fortnight, the school is likely to be quite difficult about the matter, and the headteacher might well utter remarks like, 'His education will suffer.' Elevating the importance of the school curriculum has even more sinister consequences at the secondary level. It results in labels like 'the less able younger school leaver'. And it results in pupils devaluing themselves with statements like, 'We're the thickies.' It also results in some pupils possibly according themselves a higher degree of importance than is justified in human terms simply because they are able to succeed in those areas specified as important by the school.

And the consequences of that are manifold. Some of them impinge on areas raised in the discussion about competition (below). But for the moment it can be said that one of the major consequences of the identification of education with schooling is the creation and perpetuation of social division according to the ways in which young people relate to the school curriculum. This must also be followed further when we discuss the nature of that curriculum. Here it needs simply to be stated that school achievement has a significant bearing upon a person's valuation of himself, and that any compulsory institutionalized system of valuing some people and devaluing others is inevitably socially divisive.

Of course some would maintain that divisiveness and selectivity are two sides of the same coin: while every society needs selection mechanisms to facilitate the efficient development and distribution of its members' skills, there will always be an element of divisiveness in the process; and if it was not education that was being divisive then it would be something else.

The matter of selection of gifts whose development society is institutionally committed to nurturing requires further discussion. The issue of the divisive features in society requires that we make choices about which of them we allow to be divisive and how we go about minimizing their divisive effects. At this stage we can at least say the following: because institutional education looms so important in peoples' lives it is important that those involved in this sector do all in their power to minimize its divisive ingredients.

Competition and Co-operation

Michael's parents were concerned that he should grow up to regard himself as a person with gifts and talents to share with others, and that he should regard others as people who had gifts and talents to share with him. One way in which his parents sought to help their children attain this understanding was by encouraging the family to operate in a co-operative rather than a competitive way whenever this was possible. So when the family was hurriedly getting ready to go out, and the children were having problems with jumpers and coats, they were encouraged to help one another, rather than be 'put down' by competitive statements like, 'You are slow – why can't you do it as quickly as Michael?'

One tea-time during the second week of Michael's first term at school, he hurried through his sausages and baked beans, put his fork down, and announced, 'I'm the winner.' A week later when he was talking about the books from which the school was trying to teach him to read, he said, 'I can read better than David, but I can't read as well as Angela.' Thus, within a few weeks of starting school, there were signs that the co-operative ethos of the home was being challenged by a different ethos imbibed at school, namely the competitive.

While one can understand the difficulties encountered by reception-class teachers in getting between twenty and thirty very small children to put their coats on in order to go out into the playground for a short break, or in encouraging them to eat their meal and make room for the next sitting, it is at least open to question whether competitive stimuli are the most effective and desirable. It could equally be argued that competitive 'encouragements' are either expressions of teachers' own value systems, or expressions of their occasional frustrations during the odd particularly trying time of the day. In addition, it has to be acknowledged that children pick up values from one another, and that some children are nurtured in homes that operate largely according to a competitive ethos. When they go to school, they will continue to operate in the same way. The competitive ethos of schools is reinforced by the tendency to make comparisons between pupils. This implicitly sells the notion that a person judges his achievement in a particular subject, not against outside objective standards nor in relation to his own potential, but against the people around him. Since identity and self-worth are related to achievement (compare the self-esteem of a high-flying financial whiz-kid in his ultra-modern office with that of an unemployed school leaver surveying the boards in his local job centre), and since human beings have an instinctive need and drive to be valued, it follows that, if attainment is the result of competition, then a significant number of people in the community will be significantly affected by a driving philosophy which implicitly says. 'I get my sense of worth at other people's expense.' Or to put it more crudely, 'It's either them or me.'

There would seem to be little doubt that this way of looking at things is pretty dominant in many parts of the world. The nuclear arms race is one manifestation. So is the competitiveness, both national and international, between producers of manufactured goods (not to speak of that most competitive of all industries – advertising – seeking constantly to convince people that they need things of which they are frequently not even aware). So also is regular confrontation between what competitive notions have led us to call 'the two sides of industry'. As for attitudes which are racist, or socially exclusive, like those enshrined in the rules and membership conditions of many clubs and societies for the achievers (Golf clubs? Squash clubs? Exclusive tennis clubs?), these are just the logical outcome of a dominant competitive-achieving ethic which dominates many western societies, and which men and women have been conned into believing to be 'natural' and 'normal' and 'necessary'.

Tawney has argued that it is this ethic for which Protestant Christianity must take the greatest blame. And Erich Fromm maintains that human beings cannot endure what it does to them. If they are right, then it must be that one of the greatest contributions that Christians in education can do to put right the wrongs of the past is to question competitiveness whenever it rears its head, and seek to overcome it with co-operation.

The English educational system is already itself aware that co-operative alternatives do exist which can, in the end, create a more effective learning environment in schools: primary school children working together in groups and teaching one another (there is nothing so effective for fixing in one's mind a newly learned idea as telling someone else about it), pupils in a whole class together creating art-work in the form of a mural half the length of the school corridor, the encouragement of learning music through participation in a band, or group or orchestra – all these, and many others as well, provide rich and joyful experiences in which learning is experienced as fun and a child's own self-worth is discovered through the giving and receiving of gifts and talents in relationships with others.

But, in a nation where competition dominates at all levels, there are enormous difficulties in enabling people to visualize an alternative ethic, let alone giving it tangible expression. A nation of people conditioned to operate in one way inevitably finds it well nigh impossible to be too critical of the implicit assumptions according to which it is acting, and relegates the ideas of those suggesting alternatives to the same category as those of people who advocate social, political, or economic change designed to help the less privileged. The less privileged are in some sense those who have played the game of life according to society's competitive rules, and have lost. Or they might be those against whom the cards are so heavily stacked in the first place, that they never seriously begin to try the game. In this category we might today place members of some immigrant communities, as well as the less academically able (in school terms) younger school leavers in areas of industrial decline.

Of course society doesn't want to devise alternatives – because, on the whole, the very people whose voices are heard in educational debates are those who have either succeeded within the framework of rules provided by the dominant cultural ethos, or at least have come to terms with those rules. It is hard to hear the voice of the weak and the fallen and the broken. But the New Testament evidence suggests that it is precisely for the sake of the weak and the fallen and the broken that the incarnation occurred. As Simone Weil once said, 'We must always be prepared to change sides with justice – that fugitive from the winning camp.' Therein lies the pointer to the churches' pastoral as well as their prophetic roles.

The Curriculum

When discussing the curriculum, two issues stand out: the first raises questions about the ways in which young people relate to the curriculum; the second raises questions about the range of gifts that a society, through its educational system, is institutionally committed to developing. At least in recent decades in England the secondary-school curriculum was directed towards meeting the entry requirements of the universities. The universities have set and marked the traditional school-leaving certificate examinations, and generally regarded these tests as providing criteria on which to base judgements about candidates' suitability for university places (without apparently much regard for the non-curricula factors tested by public examinations). Thus it was inevitable that grammar-school curricula should be directed towards university entrance. Secondary modern education generally took the line that it was there to provide for the less academically able pupils the best possible imitation of the grammar-school menu, taking account of the probability that its pupils were more likely than their counterparts in the grammar schools to enter manual and technical employment in due course, and would therefore require some grounding in basic technical skills.

The fallacious dichotomy between academic and technical skills is now generally recognized, and the advent of comprehensive education has attempted to provide pupils with a wide range of subject options. So one might be excused for thinking that the spectre of university entrance requirements has been exorcized.

Not so. Comprehensive schools still tend to operate, for most areas of learning, a subject-orientated philosophy. Witness the unhappiness expressed by many religious-education teachers when asked to merge their subject with others in a humanities course: the cry goes up, 'My subject has disappeared.' So, most pupils still attend classes in subject boxes. No doubt this partly reflects the needs of teachers who were taught to teach in subject boxes, and the fears of parents unable to recognize education other than in the terms in which they themselves received it. Nevertheless one wonders whether a great deal of time is not wasted by including in the curriculum subjects which have always been there, perhaps unconsciously because they always have been there. The cynical comments of most people about a great deal of the information they were given at school in the name of education speaks volumes about the relevance of the curriculum both in terms of their ability at the time to make sense of it in relation to their lives, and later to recall it when it might be useful.

There are two ways in which you deal with this: the first is by providing an integrated day to demonstrate that all knowledge is integrated and related; the second is by relating all learning to experience (recognizing that imagination is an essential part of experience). In large measure primary education has been able to achieve these objectives. But the resistance still comes at the secondary level: there, the 'body of knowledge' view still holds sway – the argument that the intrinsic essence of a subject will be compromised if it is not presented 'pure and undefiled' as it were.

Thus, those pupils with both the motivation and the kind of minds which respond to education in these terms will be those who succeed in school, go on to university, and become the next generation of leaders in society. Those who do not have that motivation and response will be the schools' failures. It could well be argued that it is precisely those who do not respond whose skills need most to be developed for the sake of society. The existing succeeders are unlikely to do other than perpetuate the implicitly held inherited values in any society. The very people in whom lies the possibility of giving expression to a new set of options are the very people given least help by school and universities.

Of course there are risks in encouraging and enabling those who disagree fundamentally with you. But equally western societies face enormous dangers in continuing along their present roads. The gods of consumerism, economic growth, and ever-increasing production – all part of the same family – are far from omnipotent. It might be that we have not yet learned to worship them properly. But it might also be the case that these gods are false gods to worship whom is to leave yourself only with a range of perceptions and options which lead ultimately to self-destruction. At least within this risky context it is worth while hedging your bets by stimulating and encouraging those who are innately more likely to experience life in all its fullness only in a society offering a package of values different from those currently on offer and whose selling is colluded with by institutionalized education. Therein lies the possibility of creating a society which is genuinely open – providing people with real options about the value systems they can adopt and by which they can choose to live their lives.

Learning to Be

Education as we have known it through all the forms of society which have lasted for any length of time has been the select instrument by means of which existing values and balances of power have been maintained and kept in effect, with all the implications of both a positive and negative character which this process has had for the destiny of nations and the course of history.[1]

The Church has always been most true to its prophetic function when it has sought to point the way, in the society in which it was set, to a better world. It has always been most true to its vocation when it has questioned cultural norms – Isaac asking his father where the ram was that he intended to offer as sacrifice, and the question leading Abraham to a new perception of the loving-kindness of God; Nathan the prophet challenging David over his behaviour with Bath-Sheba; Jesus challenging the religious of his day over the observance of the Sabbath; Paul proclaiming that Christians should not be conformed to the values of this world – rather they should be transformed by the renewing of their hearts and minds in order to know the will of God; Wilberforce insisting, 'Slavery is wrong'; Raikes insisting that all children should be given the opportunity to learn to read; Martin Luther King proclaiming the conviction that in the sight of God, and therefore in the sight of his children, all human beings are equal whatever the colour of their skin or the accident of their birth.

The Church has always been at its most significant when it has left society to preserve what was good, and given its attention to changing the evil of which society was not aware.

It is of the nature of human institutions that they will be in the business of self-preservation. While doing this, and preserving many of their good features, they will also develop demonic features because self-preservation proclaims the notion that creation is static – a notion which believers in a dynamic, creating, and redeeming God can only regard as utterly sinful. And unless the demonic is exorcized, and the institution changed and redeemed, it will surely die. Edgar Faure speaks of the 'implications of both a positive and negative character which' arise from the preservation of existing values and balances of power. The Christian community, in its concern for education and society, can leave to others the business of preserving the good: they will – there's no fear over that – provided that Christians give attention to what needs changing.

And society, using its educational system, transmits a whole variety of values which do violence to a Christian understanding of what it is to be a human being, made in the image of God, called to be an inheritor of the Kingdom of God, and thus called to be a co-creator of that Kingdom beginning here and now.

We have already alluded to the destructive effects of competition, both for individuals and for communities; we have followed through the consequences of allowing people to identify education with schooling; we have examined the consequences implicit in the selective nature of the educational curriculum. But that's not the end of it. The whole institution of education transmits a great deal more: it tells us that human beings are commodities capable of being labelled (mathematician, musician, historian, less able); it tells us that individual human beings take second place to the society of which they are a part – that they can only find fulfilment in ways which reinforce rather than threaten society as it is; it tells us that the values which we have inherited are good and right and true, and that they find adequate expression in the institutions into which it seeks to socialize us; it tells us that the only acceptable changes are those which tinker around on the surface, and that the New Testament notion of turning the world upside down – of changing the fundamental assumptions inherent in our corporate life-style – is not a viable option; it tells us that knowledge and insight are one, and by insisting that knowledge is to be transmitted from one who has it to one who doesn't, it cons us into believing that insight resides only in the one who has knowledge; it tells us that cognitive knowledge is better than aesthetic, and, by implication, it tells us that to 'know about' something is adequate and sufficient, and that it is not necessary to love as well; it tells us that inherited authority figures are good – like teachers and parents and policemen and magistrates – and it makes those of us who disagree with them from time to time feel guilty and sinful; it tells us that if we don't achieve then we deserve to be unemployed and have less opportunity to live full and abundant lives.

While there is a measure of truth in all these assertions, there is also within them a measure of untruth to which the Christian is called to draw attention: while it may be possible to say of one person, 'He has a mathematical bent to his mind', this is not all that can be said about him: he is also a totally unique individual with a whole range of other gifts to offer to and share with his fellow human beings, and to know about his mathematical bent may be to know of some of the least important things that might be discovered from being in a loving relationship with him. To tell us that the human being takes second place to the society in which he finds himself tells us something about society's need for self-preservation, but it doesn't tell us that society exists for the benefit of human beings who make it up – for all of us, including the least powerful.

Society is not threatened by those who are critical of what they find – rather, society needs their message to be spoken and their voice to be heard. Of course many of our inherited values may be good and right and true: but their institutional expression may in fact be doing violence to the values it is thought they enshrine. Of course knowledge is important, but so also is unconditioned and uncompromised insight. Of course there is a place for authority figures, but the greater is their authority the more do they need to be subjected to criticism.

As for turning the world upside down, and 'loving' as against 'knowing about', the Christian tradition has a great deal to say. The Spirit of God works in many ways. Certainly through the biblical revelation with whose help we are able to say of so many features of contemporary society, 'These are wrong'. Certainly through the churches' inherited understanding of the Christian tradition, though the diversity of views within the wider Christian community is warning enough of the subjective nature of peoples' judgements regarding which attitudes are Christian and which are not. But the Creator and Redeemer are one. And God works his redemptive activity in the post-incarnation period also through his continuing and ongoing creativity – the new spirits which arrive in the world as yet uncontaminated by social conditioning. Or, to put it another way, he always has sought to work like this, but has been prevented through existing power processes extinguishing some of those spirits before they could flourish – take the story of David with which this chapter began. And the loss was not only David's – it was society's as well. So, the role of the Christian community is threefold: first, to offer critical judgement about what is happening in society; second, to suggest solutions and alternatives; and third, to recognize that even the judgements of members of the Christian community are likely to be socially conditioned and therefore insufficiently imaginative, and thus make it necessary to stimulate and encourage the development of those free spirits still able to see visions and dream dreams without cynicism or despair.

Where Christians involved in education are seeking a vision of what their task might be, perhaps we could put it in terms of enabling a young person to take hold of and give expression in his way to this vision of full and abundant living from a loving adult to a loved child:

> Though men bind your body in rules and conventions
> Your spirit may still be free:
> Free to dream
> Free to hope
> Free to strive
> Free to love.
> Take that freedom bravely by the hand
> And let it fill your being
> Till your heart should soar
> To worlds as yet unknown to men.
> Then
> Live in the dreams that you freely see
> That you may bring them to pass for your brother.

NOTE

1 Edgar Faure, *Learning to Be: The World of Education Today and Tomorrow* (on behalf of UNESCO, 1972).

Myths–Utilities
and a Meaningful Existence
1900–1980

Philip Cliff

When the centenary of the establishment of Sunday Schools was celebrated in the year 1880, success was in the air! In the week preceding the Centenary Convention a Mr F. J. Hartley contributed to the *Sunday School Chronicle* a set of statistics on schools throughout the world.

> The progress of the Sunday School system from the day when Robert Raikes placed the first twenty children under the care of Mrs King, in the small cottage in Catherine Street, Gloucester (which still stands as a memorial of the past), to this Centennial year, when at least twelve millions of scholars are under religious instruction on the Lord's Day – has been truly marvellous, and calls forth the irresistible exclamation, 'What hath God wrought!'[1]

The article goes on to recount how in the short space of seven years the number of scholars amounted to nearly a quarter of a million. (The precise evidence for this much quoted figure is lacking, and many commentators would say that it is too high.) But more substantial figures appeared in 1818 from a Parliamentary Return which gave the number of schools as 5,463 and of Sunday scholars as 477,225, a little above four per cent of the population. A further Parliamentary Return in 1833 gave the figures as 16,828 schools and 1,548,890 Sunday scholars or almost eleven per cent of the population. The Educational Census of 1851 gave the numbers as 23,514 schools and 2,407,642 Sunday scholars or almost thirteen and one half per cent of the population. Hartley says that no authoritative records have been available since then, but he assumes that the percentage increase has been maintained and suggests that it has gone up to around fifteen per cent, which would give a figure of 3·8 millions in 1880. From other computations, he estimated a world Sunday-school population of twelve millions:

England	3,800,000	
Scotland	494,533	
Ireland	320,920	
	———	(The titles are from
United Kingdom	4,615,453	Hartley's figures and
		offer an interesting
Canada	339,943	commentary on Vic-
Colonies of Australia and New Zealand	47,862	torian church think-
	———	ing.)
Total Great Britain	5,003,258	
U.S.A.	6,504,054	
Europe	400,000	
Missionary Countries	200,000	
	———	
World Total	12,107,312	

We cannot check that estimate, except to say that we have more precise figures for the year of the centenary of the Sunday School Union when a corresponding figure for England and Wales was 4,834,148[2] though the centennial volume for the Union represents success with another image:

> If the whole body of teachers and scholars marched four abreast to the Centennial Celebrations the procession would be nearly 250 miles long. If the head of the procession were just entering St Paul's Cathedral, the tail would be just leaving Durham Cathedral.[3]

Perhaps the change from precise figures to descriptive images was due to the cracks beginning to appear in the structure. As they moved nearer to the twentieth century some bolder spirits dared to offer criticism of the existing system. An article in the *Sunday School Chronicle* for 14 September 1899 suggested that the inexorable law of progress necessitates periodic readjustment or modifications of all forms of organization to meet new conditions. The Sunday schools did not appear to have learned much from the events following the 1870 Education Act. Teaching was developing into an art, lessons were well arranged, reasonably well-equipped schools were in reach of all. Merely mechanical work was gradually being reduced to a minimum, and the children were being taught to *think*, whereas in most schools the Bible was read and explained. Superintendents should visit an efficient day school and learn how ongoing work was followed up.[4] At the Triennial National Sunday School Convention in Leeds, Dr Simon (Principal of the Yorkshire Independent (Congregational) College) opened a discussion on the training of the Sunday-school teacher:

> 'During the last half century the Sunday School had been undergoing a great change. From what had the Sunday School evolved? Fifty years ago it was an institution with religious aims although mainly occupied with doing what was now done by the School Board. But the Sunday School then accomplished very largely what it chiefly tried to accomplish to teach the young to read the Bible. It would have accomplished more if it had been able to undertake more . . . Towards what was it evolving? Into an institution the definite aim of which would be one with that of the church. The work was somewhat hampered by the defective acquaintance with the contents of the Bible.' and he outlined a course of study, with instructors, examinations and a new management structure.[5]

Dr Paton of Nottingham thought that the churches ought to put all their public rooms at the disposal of the evening institutions. H. C. Devine thought that the Sunday-school teachers underestimated the improved general knowledge, the increased prosperity and the new weeknight habits; to look at the music halls, dance saloons, was to recognize that young people were not wanted at home, but that repression was not the remedy.[5] In the correspondence and articles that followed, guilds, the Young People's Society for Christian Endeavour, the Boys' Brigade, and institutes were all suggested to rescue young people from aimlessness. Dr Fairbairn, the eminent theologian, thought that the better training of teachers was needed; Dr George Adam Smith thought likewise and that a more discriminating use of the Bible ought to be insisted upon. Professor Alfred Wallace said:

> I do not rate the Sunday School highly. In my opinion they were merely a temporary panacea against ignorance and overwork in the early days of the factory system . . . I consider that if Sunday School teachers took their pupils into the field or garden and showed them some of the beauty and interest and mystery of nature, more good would be done than by all the Sunday Schools I have ever heard of.[6]

Dr F. Clark (of the YPSCE) thought there ought to be more emphasis on spiritual teaching and less on the history, geography, and archaeology of the Bible. But the biblicists came back on that:

> Changes are impending in the general constitution and methods of the Sunday School, and those most zealous for their efficiency are the least hostile to their full discussion. The Sunday School of the future must be more and more the Bible Teaching Institute of the Church. It must fasten upon Holy Scripture with all its strength and teach the Gospel powerfully and clearly to every scholar. This is its real function. The educational and recreational elements are incidental to its greatest work and are to be prized only as far as they advance it. And their knowledge of the Gospel must be experimental. For long years our schools have been working on these lines. The future will see them more and more recognizing this as their divinely appointed ministry.[7]

In the same issue the topics for 1900 were outlined. The morning lessons for the year traversed more or less continuously the First and Second Books of Samuel, and in the afternoon 'Aspects of Jesus' Ministry'. Later that month there was a discussion on why morning school was declining so rapidly.[8] The writers put it down to 'godless homes, late Saturday nights, love of pleasure, the new fresh air philosophy and weekend trips'. It could not possibly be that First and Second Samuel were irrelevant to 1900!

In August of 1900 a Mr Howard Evans presented some Sunday-school statistics that showed there had been a decline of 30,000 in the previous year, as the population had risen by 300,000. The newspapers took this up. Some of them saw attendance too much as a mark of a particular social class. There was need for more joyousness and brightness, the teaching needed broadening and improving. Others felt that too much was being made of the decline, many of the Senior scholars, they thought, had moved into S.P.S.A.s, Y.M.C.A.s, institutes, and the like. Correspondence suggested that class teaching was falling off. There were problems about the status of the school in relationship to the Church, and problems of the status of teachers too.[9] Carey Bonner (the General Secretary of the Sunday School Union) said that on every hand the schools were not retaining the hold they formerly had on senior scholars.[10] The Church of England reported a slight decrease in their 1899 numbers, but no perceptible diminution of interest.[11] The Congregational Union thought that the statistics were too reliable to be set on one side. They indicated a real decline in attractiveness, the organization was no longer to be sought after for secular education purposes; as an educational agency it had not marched with the times; the absence of the middle class depresses the social tone; consciousness of maturity comes earlier to the new generation; they had done with school and there was a new sense of seeking the love of pleasure. Others thought the bicycle was robbing our schools.[12] The Revd Hugh Price Hughes, a senior Methodist minister, agreed with the figures. 'Far more serious than the Sunday-school authorities realize,' he said.[13] The Methodist New Connexion spokesman thought 'the home must be partly to blame, since education became compulsory and free many parents had become indifferent.' He thought grading was defective too.[14] Dr P. T. Forsyth thought there had been too much coaxing with treats and prizes, and the children tended to go to the highest bidder. There was also a vast difference between Sunday-school premises and the newer school buildings. There was a growing difference between the amateur and professional teacher, lesser people often ran the Sunday schools.[15] There is growing doubt about parts of the Bible. There was a lack of worship and sense of worthwhileness and increasing varieties of Christian effort.[16] The Birmingham Sunday School Union ran a whole series of articles in its *Monthly Record* in which additional to the reasons advanced earlier, they saw some social changes – 'young people beginning to earn their livings earlier, parents were allowing wage-earning children more licence, and that there were new facilities for weekend excursions'.[17] They also recorded 'poor grading', 'many of our schools have gone down through sheer lack of interest', 'children were not always sure of having a teacher', and 'the quality of teaching was poor'.[18] The death of Queen Victoria in 1901 released much pent-up feeling and the exodus from 'the schools on Sunday' developed from a trickle to a flood. According to figures recently assembled[19] the highwater mark in Sunday-school membership came to the denominations thus:

1904	The Congregational Union Schools	734,986
1905	The Presbyterian Church of England	89,558
	The Bible Christian Church	47,242
1906	The Baptist Union	586,601
	The Methodist New Connexion	88,042
	The Primitive Methodist Church	477,114

	The United Methodist Church	194,862
	The Wesleyan Methodist Church	1,013,391
1910	The Church of England	2,437,000

There were occasional years when churches were able to report minor rises but there were more falls than rises and over the years to the present the statistics present a continuous and sustained decline of between five and six per cent per year.

It would be useful if we could point to one set of facts or circumstances and say 'these are responsible for the decline', but one cannot do that. There is no simple answer but a series of interlocking circumstances that, taken together, produced the change.

The first factor was the gradual ending of the established 'folk myth' that 'everybody had to go to Sunday school for education'. The idea had been inherited from parents to children over ten generations. Grandparents to parents to children had passed on the message that it was necessary to go to the Sunday school for a full life of learning, leisure, and eternal life. Such notions die hard, for the success of the movement was the provision of a rich subculture which, it is often suggested, created 'the respectable working class'. School on Sunday was the price to be paid for the weeknight courses, saving clubs, burial societies, sewing gatherings (where materials were provided cheaply and where sewing machines were provided), sports events, libraries, mutual improvement societies, and many more activities out of which many secular concerns had also arisen: trade-union activity, interest in local and national politics and so forth. It was only in the three generations after 1870 that some began to realize that one need not endure the Sunday session to have the subculture.

The movement institutionalized its former success. It could not possibly be that there was anything wrong with an institution which had grown continuously year by year since 1780! In all this one must not denigrate what had been done. Over a long period of years, elementary education had been given to many. A vast literature had been produced from spelling lists, lesson helps, reward and literary books, to a weekly newspaper. Apart from the newspaper, the Anglican and Free Church peoples had received much from their own printing presses. Methods of educational technique had been examined and the works of people like David Stow, Henry Dunn, James Gall, and the monitorial systems of Lancaster and Bell had been commented upon. Lectures, libraries, and even a Reading Room (in London) open daily had been provided. Bible reading schemes such as that of the International Bible Reading Association had been prepared and sold. Training 'colleges' or 'institutes' had been set up for the enthusiastic teachers to learn by correspondence and examination. Special music, tune-books and hymnbooks brought into being, and World Conventions for Sunday-school workers (the first world ecumenical gatherings in the post-Reformation era) set up, and there had been much philanthropic work both national and local introduced. The Sunday School Union had its first Holiday Homes in 1886 and locally many children were helped to country days, seaside visits, and 'bun fights' over a long period of time. 'At homes', 'soirées', Good Friday conferences, choral gatherings, public speaking contests all helped to create a sense of the significance and importance of the work. Lord Mayors, mayors, councillors, peers of the realm, and Members of Parliament all vied with one another in telling the world that they taught in Sunday school. But by the third generation after 1870 many of the young had come to realize that it no longer mattered and allowed themselves to succumb to the delights of bicycles, cheap railway fares, dances, music halls, and such like 'temptations'. The people were gradually ceasing to be 'puritan' in outlook and desire, and as the Sunday school ceased to be the means of secular education so it became easier to leave an institution that outwardly still spoke for more stringent ways of life. The *Sunday School Chronicle*, for instance, still sought pledges for non-smoking, total abstinence, anti-gambling, and for seeking to keep the art galleries, parks, and museums closed on the Sabbath.

There were movements threatening to undermine the hitherto unchallenged assumptions about the inerrancy of the Scriptures. From the time when the Bible was the chief reading book, to the post-1870 Act period of Bible teaching and Scripture examinations, etc., the Sunday school had had as its prize and treasure the Bible. When the movement ceased to teach reading, it taught the Bible as its overall objective and provided the Scripture examination as the evaluative mark for good teaching. The 'infection' from Darwinism and the German schools of higher and lower biblical criticism of the Bible tended to divide people, setting sons against fathers, so that 'a man's foes were those of his own household'.

The movement had, for the most part, been a layman's movement.

Many had learned in its midst how to conduct meetings, take minutes, speak in public, so that it became a way of life that held meaning for them. To examine, as I have done, old minute books, reports, accounts of schools and associated bodies such as local unions is to see a continuity of names and office-bearers, to see year after year people being recommended to the parent Union for long-service diplomas for anything up to fifty years of continuous service. The Sunday-school movement provided perhaps the chief outlet for lay talent. The new schools of thought about the Bible, however, were mainly ministerial and this constituted a second threat. Another strand in the folk tradition is that ordinary Sunday-school teachers know best what children need. 'They need to know the Bible!' As though knowing the Bible from cover to cover would produce saints! Some of the men who criticized the way the Bible was being used were scholars like Professor Peake and S. R. Driver, Drs Fairbairn and Garvie to name but a few, but happily they not only attacked an unbending literalism, they worked for the teaching of the newer understandings of the Bible. Dr Garvie and his colleagues carried on the warfare through lectures, letters to the press, articles in religious magazines.[20] To take to 'a higher criticism which discredited the verbal inspiration of the Bible [was] a hard knock for Protestant-ism'.[21] It was even more so for the Sunday schools – for whom the Bible was Pope. At this point the Anglicans, at least those in the Tractarian or high-church tradition, were in a slightly better position since the Tractarian emphasis on the framework of the faith en-shrined in the creeds and the sacred tradition 'liberated them from bibliolatry this is, from an exclusive dependence on the letter of the Scripture as the only source of revelation'.[22] The right of every man to interpret the Scriptures as he sees them provides for some a sublime certainty, not to say even bigotry, but also goes a long way to destroying the very thing it wishes most of all to offer – a secure faith in the gospel. The brash certainties of a secular scientific dogmatism were more attractive to many than the dogmatisms of the biblical fundamentalists. It is significant that the losses of children occurred, and to a large extent still occur, in the age ranges of 10 to 14 as children move from concrete to abstract thinking and question their hitherto unchallenged assumptions.

The majority of schools were poor in accommodation, equipment, and in skilled teachers, and they were mostly ungraded. Some had attempted to remove the youngest children from 'the school' but not all. Robert Denholm, a former General Secretary of the then National Sunday School Union, reminisced in the year of his Presidency of the Union (1952) back over fifty years.

My first superintendency was a Methodist Mission Hall in a slum area in Brixton, prior to the First World War (actually in 1903). There were about 250 children – tough guys we would call them today – and a staff of 20, a totally ungraded school like all other Sunday Schools in those days far away and long ago. The staff were a mixed bag – as all staffs are. As a young schoolmaster I realized that something needed to be done to sort things out, so as to improve the discipline and make the teaching effective. For a year I cultivated their friendship and ruled in affection. I then suggested we should grade the school. They were at first aghast, but our love for each other and mutual trust in one another made it possible, and on the first Sunday in 1904, the surgical and spiritual operation was performed. There were many tears, but they gave way to happy laughter when I impishly announced the next hymn:

> Here we suffer grief and pain,
> Here we meet to part again,
> In Heaven we part no more.

This was three years before Hamilton Archibald had got going.[23]

The debate about grading went on for many years. One of the major denominations was still debating whether grading was the cause of the decline in the number of scholars in 1938! One can still find schools where there is still little or no grading.

It is salutary to pause and reflect on the different understanding we have about children today, their growing and learning processes, compared with our understandings at the turn of the century. Changes were brought about by a close study of the way in which children grow, develop, and learn following the insights pioneered by people like Froebel, Starbuck, Hall, and popularized in this country by George Hamilton Archibald. Today he would be described as a 'charismatic figure' who appeared like an answer to the prayers of many earnest souls. Indeed Dr R. F. Horton, a leading theologian of the period and not given to undeserving praise, said 'I believe God raised him up to lead the whole Christian Church into a fuller and more scientific management of this great agency (the

Sunday school) for his Kingdom.'[24] His life story, which can only be briefly mentioned here, is told by his daughter in her book *George Hamilton Archibald – Crusader for Youth*.[25] His contribution to church education is told in more detail by Ralph Newman in his Robert Raikes Historical Society's Annual Lecture for 1957.[26] S. Allen Warner has catalogued the growth of the Graded School Movement up to 1913,[27] and Archibald's contribution to the work of the British Lessons Council is documented in Hill's *Pioneering for Christ* in his 1966 Lecture.[28] A brief Memorial booklet was published on his death in 1938 by the Council of Westhill College, which institution he founded in 1907, and is still his permanent memorial.[29]

Archibald was born in Halifax, Nova Scotia, in 1858, went into business and in his spare time involved himself in Sunday school for fifteen years. He was caught up with the new schools of method, then being developed in the United States at Chatauqua (a lakeside camping and conference centre in New York State). By 1895 he was so involved that he sold out his share in the family business and took his family with him to Springfield, Mass., where he embarked on a two-year diploma course at the School for Christian Workers. (The School was later moved to Hartford, Conn., from where he received an honorary degree of D.D. for his services to Christian education in 1933.) Having graduated he returned to Canada to become the Provincial Secretary to the Quebec Sunday School Association. There his skills as a lecturer, his years of practical experience, his sense of humour, and his ability to persuade people to change their methods of work made him exceedingly popular as a speaker. He came on a private visit to Britain in 1902, met with the Revd Carey Bonner, the then General Secretary of the Sunday School Union, and the accord was so great that he was engaged as an extension lecturer. His great contribution was to help people to 'see' children as they had never seen them before. As one early commentator put it:

He holds that very much Sunday School activity is ineffective not because teachers as a whole do not study the Bible, but because they know next to nothing of the scholars. Knowledge of children, and the sympathy which is the fruit of such knowledge, give the essential key to success. He further holds that one source of vital weakness in English Sunday Schools lies not so much in any lack of willingness or ability to teach on the part of the workers as in the lack of any teacher-producing plant. For the solution of this and other practical problems of Sunday School organization Mr Archibald has his own clear and practical suggestions. He is a man with a constructive programme.

A remarkable feature of his work is the attraction which he possesses for day school teachers and for parents of all classes. In Halifax and Barry, the elementary school teachers in a body attended practically every lecture. The educational authorities there, as in many other places, shortened school hours to allow of the attendance of the teachers at the afternoon conferences.[30]

The programme of lectures that drew regular audiences of between three and four thousand people was in summary form:

LECTURE 1. DIFFERENCES IN CHILDREN

The disobedient child. The restless child. The quiet child. Children's dress.

LECTURE 2. THE WORLD OF MAKE BELIEVE

Stories, Myths, Legends, Fairy Tales, The Santa Claus Question. Children's Lies. Sand piles, Blocks, Toys, Blackboards, etc.

LECTURE 3. THE COMMONEST THING IN THE WORLD

The power of suggestion. The secret of keeping order.

LECTURE 4. THE ACTIVE CHILD

How to keep a child out of mischief. The use of the play instinct. Activities in the Sunday School. The Child and the Sabbath. Through muscles to the heart.

LECTURE 5. ADOLESCENCE

LECTURE 6. RIGHT AND WRONG PUNISHMENTS

Training the Will. The right use of fear. The duty of becoming useless.

LECTURE 7. ORGANIZATION AND GRADING OF THE SUNDAY SCHOOL

How to get teachers. How to hold our elder scholars. The re-organized Infant Class.[31]

Warner indicates that some fifty or so books were produced in the first ten or so years of the century taking up the child-study theme and its implications for the Sunday school. But not only the lectures, it was also the Easter Conferences for Sunday School Workers, through which the new insights were gradually given a deepened place in Sunday-school thinking. Demonstrations of practical work, opportunity to question the speakers, and the time to sit down together and to understand in local situations what Archibald meant when he quoted, and requoted the great saying of Froebel 'Wouldst thou teach a child? Observe him, he will tell you what to do.' Archibald lectured at the Woodbrooke Conference in 1905, and later that year Mr Archibald and his daughter, challenged by Mr George Cadbury to put the theories into practice, set up a model Sunday school in Bournville. Visitors came in their hundreds to see the ideas in operation. The full story of those days is told in Ethel Johnston's life of her father.[32]

Following the Woodbrooke Easter Conference, the lecture tours continued up and down the country. The Conferences continued, Southport, Southend, Scarborough, Bournville, Westminster, Harrogate, Swanwick, and Swanwick again in 1913. The Conference aimed at drawing in people from a wide area and in gradually covering the country. In the years after the War the Westhill Easter Conference at Swanwick became the training ground for hundreds and hundreds of young Sunday-school teachers and the centre for a fellowship of dedicated people across the country. Archibald's dream of a 'Training Institute for Christian Workers', such as he had known at the Hartford Seminary became a reality in 1907 through the generosity of Geraldine and Barrow Cadbury who, spurred on by the vision of what Archibald was doing, promised to stand by such an experiment for three years with financial support. A house was found in Selly Oak close by Kingsmead, called 'West Hill' which would accommodate twelve students, and so the experiment began. A small day school was started so that the students would have daily opportunity for child study, and a Froebel Teacher Training Department was set up so that those who were to train for work in the Church and Sunday school should be as proficient as those in day school. For over seventy years this objective has been pursued and the College has never been without students for 'Sunday-school work'. The Anglicans (in terms of personalities, Miss Hetty Lee of Manchester High School worked very closely with Mr Archibald) were likewise moved to share the enthusiasm of the new movement. Miss Lee was appointed as the National Organizer of Sunday School Work by the National Society and in

1908 they started their equivalent of Westhill at St Christopher's, Blackheath.

The new interest in child study could not but reflect itself in a new look at lesson material. Up to 1909 there were no published 'graded lessons' although the need for them was growing. By 1907 it was estimated that some 600 schools had done major reorganization and by 1908 the figure had risen to about 1,500. Some schools were using Archibald's *Bible Lessons for Little Beginners*, and others were turning to American material. A high-level conference was organized by the Sunday School Union between biblical scholars and Sunday-school experts, which urged that the results of biblical criticism should be put plainly and convincingly before the teachers; then that for the efficient instruction and training of young people 'it is absolutely necessary that the principles of grading should have fuller recognition . . . than at present accorded to it; that the International Lesson System should be remodelled to bring it more into line with the needs of the modern Sunday school; and that clergy and ministers should see to it that some competent person arrange for training classes in each church; and that some training should be given to theological students.[33] Thus eventually graded materials emerged. First through a new magazine *Teachers and Taught*, begun in 1909 with separate courses for beginners (aged four and five), primary (aged six, seven, and eight), junior (aged eight to twelve) and senior (for twelve and over). Then the *Sunday School Chronicle* started to provide weekly graded notes in addition to notes on the Uniform Lessons. The National Society of the Church of England also began its own Scheme in 1910.[34]

By 1915, those involved in the discussions between the British and American Lessons Committees found themselves unable to agree on further co-operative work, and so the British Lessons Council came into being in 1916. It consisted of eight educationalists, eight Sunday-school experts, seventeen denominational representatives, and six biblical scholars. They saw to it that the biblical materials were appropriate to the age groups and that the biblical material incorporated the insights of biblical scholarship, as far as was possible. They published Annual Lists, called for writers, drafts of work for each department, and made their work available to the denominations for use and publication. These publications were variously known as *Concise Guides*, *Graded Teacher*, *Teachers and Taught*, and the weekly notes in the *Sunday School Chronicle*. In all this Mr Archibald played a leading role. He remained the Principal of Westhill, giving his services without any charge to the College, until 1930. He died in 1938.

The problems of 'institutionalized success' are many! They avoid discussions about 'utility', aims and objectives, etc., and allow only for minor changes. Raikes provided an initial pattern which was taken up and used for many purposes. Those who were genuinely concerned about educating people to read, write, and to become numerate, offering also an insight into a moral and respectable ordering of society were one group, and in a sense their work came to an end with the coming of the day schools. The Evangelicals saw in this Sunday instruction the opportunity to use the teaching of reading for the furthering of biblical awareness and knowledge. The Act of 1870, setting up elementary compulsory education in this country, gave these their big opportunity, but the tragedy of narrow appeal to the Bible alone is that it tends to be too cerebral, too dependent on memorizing Scripture, too 'spiritual' one might say, since reviewing the literature of the period one seldom if ever sees the application of biblical insights to the everyday work. To return to an earlier theme, I and II Samuel may make good reading for an adult – with due reflection an adult might discover permanent truth for today – but to expect that children should know I and II Samuel for their own sake, was asking too much, but few questioned the programme. The morning school began to go down and down, and by the 1920s few remained, which left the Sunday-school children now meeting in the afternoon, often in a different building from 'the church' and meeting people whom they knew as 'my teacher' rather than as 'church members'. Another folk myth is that the Sunday schools have ever been the nursery of the Church. This has hardly ever been so, and certainly not in the present century. Information here is not too easy to come by, but I have worked over the Birmingham Sunday School Union Annual Returns for fifty years. In them churches were asked to give their numbers of children, adults, etc., and the number of those from the Sunday school who became members of the church. In only one year out of the fifty examined did the percentage reach one per cent (that is less than one in every hundred on the books). Many church members had been in the Sunday school but not all Sunday-school scholars became church members. When a Commission looked at this question in *Sunday Schools To-day*[35] in 1957, the figure then arrived at was an average of two and one half per cent (nationally). But again, looking through the material of the period there was little stress on things like church membership. If it was expected as an objective that children would become church members then in the Free Church setting it was never made explicit. One could make a strong case that the interdenominational nature of the extra-biblical material worked against any specific claims of membership. 'Church was just the other place where the other people went to at the other time' to quote a notable remark of H. A. Hamilton.

H. A. Hamilton,[36] the third of the great names in the Sunday-school world, spent some of his time in the 1930s as a keen observer of the Sunday-school scene when numbers were falling and the best gains of the Archibald era were beginning to be institutionalized as 'success'. Hamilton asked questions which had not been asked for a long time: 'What is Sunday school for?', 'How do people learn?' and 'How can we harness the best insights of sociology, social psychology, etc., to help us fulfil our task?' Hamilton had served a church in Lancashire from 1924 to 1929 in which there was a typical all-age Sunday school of over 700 men, women, and children, with a staff of 70, 'and this', as he once told me 'made a considerable impression on a young minister of what a community can be':[37]

> It was the centre of those people's lives in so many ways. There was a Mutual Aid Society, dramatics, an operatic society, Billiards Club, and a Sports field. This group was the centre of their lives in all kinds of ways – their total social life. They all lived within a mile – no, less than that – most of them within a few hundred yards from this church . . . So it was a natural community that from this point of view had its focus in this set of buildings. Of course in Lancashire in those days, I felt that everyone was of the same class. Some had more money than others, but they all had the same kind of outlook, spoke to each other in the same kind of language, and wanted the same things. Now – I'd never seen this before.[38]

But a rich benefactor had provided a new cathedral-like building on the other side of the road, not at all appropriate, and Hamilton felt at first that it was his educational purpose to get the people who congregated on the one side of the road (Sunday-school premises) to join the people who congregated on the other side of the road (the church). But it did not work.

I am bound to say that I think the failure of the Church to identify itself with the social purposes of the community in the Sunday school was as much as anything the explanation of its failure. This expressed an attitude of mind, a separateness which was alien to the Gospel . . . that experience . . . really sowed the seed.[39]

Raikes had seen the need to take the children to church because this was the social pattern, the next group of educators had seen the need of presenting the children to the church on an anniversary in order to ask for 'a good collection on account of the good work you see before you'. Hamilton saw the church as the community which expressed values and thereby becomes the ideal setting for education. Thus he began to work out with his friends a scheme whereby the educational purposes of the church could be worked out in the setting of the church's life and worship. The pattern became called 'Family Church':

'Family Church' starts by assuming one Church which includes the last baptized (or dedicated) baby and the oldest saint, in one living fellowship of mutual, loving, and caring relationships. It assumes a membership that cares for its children not merely as *prospective* church members but as individuals: a spiritual home which includes both the nursery and the drawing room, and in which – as in any home worthy of the name – the children are as much at home in the drawing room as they are in the nursery: the grown-ups are often found down on the carpet sharing the children's interests, intelligently, sympathetically, and constructively. It is the Church, i.e. the living personal relationships that are the Church – which educates a child for churchmanship.[40]

The coming of the Second World War hindered the process of sharing this vision of how children could grow into faith and the arrival of 'Youth Work' in the period after the war likewise hindered the sharing.

Again, new social insights demanded new educational techniques and the Hadow Report, with its emphasis on the curriculum being seen in terms of activity rather than of knowledge, provided a new tool that Hamilton and his inner group used to create *The Christian Education Handbooks*.[41] Here learning was not seen as the transferring of little packets of facts from one mind to another, but through discovery, curiosity, putting children in the situation where they can ask questions rather than be 'just talked to', could make their own reality behind the words. The ideas behind 'Family Church' crossed many boundaries and took root in all the churches. The Methodists had their Commission and produced a series of documents, *The Way Ahead*, the Congregationalists (Hamilton was a Congregationalist) commended *Family Church in Principle and Practice*;[42] the Presbyterians produced *Children and the Church – A Handbook*[43] and the Baptists had their scheme too.

The Church of England took hold of the concept in its own way, some of the controlling ideas being seen in their understanding of 'The Parish Eucharist' or 'Family Communion'. In *Confirmation Today*[44] and *Towards the Conversion of England*[45] some disturbing facts had come to light which pointed to a like failure within the system of transmitting 'the tradition' to future generations:

> The figures for the past are not very encouraging: 67 per cent of the children of our country are baptized at our fonts, 34 per cent attend our Sunday instructions, 26 per cent are confirmed, 9 per cent receive Communion at Easter, and a far smaller percentage become regular communicants.[46]

The literature for the movement within the Church of England is considerable[47] and it helped the Church to come to terms with the world of the fifties and sixties.

'Goldman', a word that still produces a chill down the spine of many, spells out the surname of one who 'troubled Israel' when she was ready to settle down again to routinized complacency. Goldman sought to explore whether the theories of Piaget, in regard to children's learning, were the same for religious education as they appeared to be for mathematical education. He discovered a scientific basis for Archibald's intuitive approach to grading;[48] but more – that religious *thinking* did not reach real depth and fullness until a young person had reached mature abstract thinking or 'the stage of formal operational thinking'. The way in which this research was misheard is interesting. It was rejected by those who thought what was being said was that no religious education could take place until a child was fourteen or fifteen! It was accepted by those who did not want to do religious education in day school! Goldman had been talking about only one aspect of learning, namely the cognitive approach, but there are other ways of knowing and of learning, through the affective approach, and here what one 'feels' about people, about places, is important. Attitudes are anchored in groups, and attitudes are not made nor changed by reason alone. To those who settled down quietly with what Goldman was saying, who came back to the Froebelian 'Watch the child', a new insight into curriculum development emerged. Once the lessons of Hubery[49] and Goldman[50] had been digested a new syllabus 'Experience and Faith' was produced by the British Lessons Council in 1967. From that syllabus a new publication *Partners in Learning*[51] emerged for the Free Churches. A likeminded group within the Church of England produced a series of books for the different age groups called *Alive in God's World*.[52] The Church of Scotland produced their own material based upon the new insights *Growing Up in the Church*.[53] All the material has had its enthusiastic advocates, and its devastating critics! The watershed for the most part is still either 'There is too much Bible' or 'There is not enough of the Bible in it'. It would be a great pity if we hardened along these lines for in a way both need insight and listening to. Of course one wants to know the Bible as the great truth revealer, but one wants to be aware first of encountering the God who makes the people whose book the Bible is.

> We use the mono-syllable 'GOD' very easily. It means nothing as a sound: the sound is the symbol of what reality is to us. If you want to know what G-O-D is really like to you; ask yourself what you want most in life. What you want most in life is the thing in which you are, in fact, believing, which is, in fact, controlling your choices and decisions and desires. It is only when the symbol 'God' does represent to us Jesus, so that we can say God is Love, God is Personal, God is like Jesus, that we have a Christian faith in God.
> A living Christian Faith is not learned by heart. It is set down for us in the symbols of words, in the creeds and practices of worship in the church, but it is not so communicated to us.[54]

Once that encounter through persons has taken place, even I and II Samuel may have something to impart to us! But, to tell a Bible story is so much easier than to find imaginative ways of sharing encounter with 'the Beyond in the midst'! Perhaps because preaching has been the only means of sharing the truth for many, preaching to children is still the only way to know – or trust. Just as 'the "Word of God" is not bound' so Christian learning cannot be routinized, institutionalized, enfolded in the pages of a book – it can only come alive through loving persons.

Today, two hundred years after Robert Raikes's 'little experiment', we have come full circle. Insights into the socialization process have made us aware of the part the family must play in the transmission of culture, religion, and life style. We have become aware through many studies that there is a direct correlation between churchgoing parents and church membership. That just as parents and grandparents have a part to play in helping a child to know his own history, to receive a tradition, a family name, that is honourable and meaningful; that the home creates us as persons, the village or town gives us a heritage, and our county a geographical existence to be proud of (or not – depending on the results of county cricket matches!) so a religious community has its part to play in our growth to full mature faith. It is from the church community that we receive the experience that makes real the language of religion, from the people of the church we receive a life style, through the community's story a spiritual history and inheritance. We need the family, the community, and the community's book. We need to know and to feel the relevance and importance of the community for our security, but it must be a living community, a generational thing, personalized and sincere. Thus our worship and work must have utility. Raikes's plan succeeded because it had utility, it offered something valuable, real; in the post-1870 period the Bible had utility as long as one believed that the words were the Word; if that insight has changed have we not still to give the most precious gift of loving people into the Kingdom through meaningful centres of abundant life? Utility is not found by routinization nor institutionalization but through a fresh encounter with him who makes all things new.

NOTES

1 *The Centenary of Sunday Schools 1880. A Memorial of the Celebration* (London, Sunday School Union, 1881), pp. 8–12.

2 It is not easy to accept the statistics of the period because the Union statistics sometimes include figures for other Unions such as the Indian S.S.U. and not the Anglican figures. The total for the Free Church bodies in England and Wales, but only for the Anglican provinces of Canterbury and York, would be 5,334,146.

3 *The Hundredth Year. The Story of the Centenary of the Sunday School Union, 1903* (London, Sunday School Union, 1903), p. 42.

4   *Sunday School Chronicle* (1899), p. 536.

5   Op. cit., p. 659.

6   Op. cit., p. 746.

7   *Sunday School Chronicle* (1900), p. 18.

8   Op. cit., p. 45.

9   Op. cit., p. 631.

10   Op. cit., p. 675.

11   Op. cit., p. 661.

12   Loc. cit.

13   Op. cit., p. 729.

14   Op. cit., p. 767.

15   Op. cit., p. 849.

16   Loc. cit.

17   *Birmingham Sunday School Union Monthly Record*, April 1901, p. 55, and February 1902, p. 18.

18   Op. cit., 1901, p. 15, and February 1902, p. 18.

19   R. Currie, A. Gilbert, and L. Horsley, *Church and Churchgoers. Patterns of Church Growth in the British Isles since 1700.* Oxford U. P. 1977. A most valuable research tool.

20   A. E. Garvie became Principal of New College, Hampstead, in 1906. It was largely through his foresight, keenness, and wisdom that a large number of the scholars, theologians, and other experts threw their weight behind the Movement for Sunday School Reform. He became the first Chairman of the British Lessons Council.

21   A. J. P. Taylor, *English History 1914–1945* (Oxford, 1965), p. 168.

22   Horton Davies, *Worship and Theology in England from Watts and Wesley to Maurice* (Princeton U. P. 1961), p. 257.

23   *Sunday School Chronicle*, 23 October 1952. A brief Report on Robert Denholm's Presidential Address.

24   *George Hamilton Archibald. A Memorial Document* (Westhill 1938), p. 3. o.p.

25   E. Johnston, *George Hamilton Archibald – Crusader for Youth.* Wallington, R.E.P., 1945. o.p.

26   R. T. Newman, *George Hamilton Archibald and the Beginning of the Graded School Movement.* The Robert Raikes Historical Society's Annual Lecture for 1957. London, N.S.S.U., 1957. o.p.

27   S. A. Warner, *The Growth of the Graded Sunday School.* London, Headley Brothers, 1913. o.p.

28   Clifford M. Jones, *Pioneering in Christian Education, 50 Years of the British Lessons Council.* Jubilee Lecture. Wallington, R.E.P., 1966. o.p.

29   Westhill College, Selly Oak, Birmingham. The College still has a section of its work concerned with Christian education.

30   *George Hamilton Archibald. A Memorial Document*, p. 5.

31   Op. cit., p. 6.

32 E. Johnston, op. cit., pp. 94ff.
33 Op. cit., pp. 89ff.
34 Op. cit., p. 104; *George Hamilton Archibald. A Memorial Document*, p. 9; S. A. Warner, op. cit., pp. 84ff.
35 *Sunday Schools Today*. Free Church Federal Council, 1957. o.p.
36 Hamilton, Herbert Alfred. Born 1897. Military Service in World War I. Lancashire Congregational College 1920–24. Bachelor of Arts (Mancr). Bolton 1924–29. Soho Hill, Birmingham 1929–33. Secretary to the Congregational Union Youth and Education Dept. 1933–45. Principal of Westhill College 1945–54. Union Church, Brighton 1954–63. Associate General Secretary of the World Council of Christian Education 1963–65. Associate General Secretary of the World Council of Churches 1965–66. Died 1977.
37 From a tape-recording of a conversation with him on the origins of Family Church. Cf. P. B. Cliff, *Family Church, its Origins, its Present and its Future*. Robert Raikes Historical Society Lecture, 1972. o.p.
38 Further extract of the tape, see n.37.
39 See n.37.
40 *Sunday School Chronicle*, 19 February 1942. 'A new slogan – Education in the Church, for the Church, by the Church'. The Revd Eric Hodgson BD, one of the collaborators with Hamilton.
41 The Christian Education Handbooks. A series of lesson materials for a nine-year cycle of work, and a complete breakthrough in curriculum development at the time. It involved a spiral curriculum of three sets of concentric courses, so that out of the materials Family Festivals at Christmas, Easter, Whitsuntide, and Summer might be worked out. The original edition was published by R.E.P. and a revision of the material later published by The Independent Press. o.p.
42 *Family Church in Principle and Practice* was the original handbook which Hamilton wrote for the Congregationalists. It ran through several editions from the original edition produced by R.E.P. in 1941. o.p.
43 All the major demonstrations produced working materials for their constituencies. The Methodists produced *The Way Ahead* over several years, developing Family Church insights into all the departments of the Junior Church, through to suggestions about youth and adult material. 1961.
    The Presbyterian Church of England document *Children and the Church* came out in 1959.
44 *Children Adrift*. London, C. of E. Council for Education. Press and Publications Board, 1949. o.p.
    S. M. Gibbard, *Tomorrow's Church*. London, National Society/SPCK, 1950. o.p. Brother Edward, *Sunday Morning – A New Way*, SPCK, 1938, publicized the early beginnings of the Parish Communion. It was taken up by Fr Gabriel Hebert in *The Parish Communion* (1957) and commended through the Parish and People Movement within the Church of England. Special Report in 1962: *The Parish Communion Today*, SPCK, 1962.
45 *Confirmation Today* was a schedule attached to interim reports presented to the Convocation of the Church of England in 1944.

46 *Towards the Conversion of England*. A Report on Evangelism presented to the Convocation of 1945. London, Church Information Office. o.p.

47 R. J. Goldman, *Religious Thinking from Childhood to Adolescence*. London, R.K.P., 1964; and *Readiness for Religion*, R.K.P. 1965.

48 Archibald had come to his conclusions about grading through close observation and an intuitive awareness that seemed to work. Goldman confirmed Archibald's findings by scientific research.

49 The Revd Douglas Hubery had been on the staff at Westhill (with Goldman) and had developed what he had called 'experiential' ways of working with children: *The Experiential Approach to Christian Education*, N.C.E.C. 1960; and *Teaching the Christian Faith Today*, N.C.E.C. 1965. He became the General Secretary of the Methodist Church's Division of Youth and Education.

50 *Experience and Faith* – A Christian Education Syllabus with parallel themes for all-age groups in the Church. British Lessons Council Methodist Youth Dept/NCEC/REP, 1967.

51 The dated yearly volumes of material for all departments, published from the Syllabus above.

52 Published by the Church Information Office and prepared by the Wadderton Group. Undated annual volumes for three-year cycle.

53 Material published by the Church of Scotland, undated for a three-year cycle.

54 H. A. Hamilton, *The Foundations of a Modern Sunday School* (London, NSSU, 1946), p. 4.

Many of the 'out of print' books, pamphlets, and other papers can be seen at Westhill's collection of research material related to the Sunday school. The Robert Raikes Historical Society's collection of material is housed there. Westhill would be glad to receive any manuscripts, old books, medals, old teaching materials, photographs of historic significance, etc., for a history of the Sunday school.

Prison Education

Alan Baxendale

This chapter* opens with a statement of the arrangements which are made nowadays for the education of people who are detained in our Prison Service establishments (prisons, remand centres, borstals, and detention centres). The statement is couched in general terms: what actually happens in individual establishments is likely to be a variation of it, depending very largely on local needs and circumstances. The chapter then continues with an historical account of the way these arrangements have evolved which, however, is not a history of education amongst people in custody. Such a history has yet to be written. All that is attempted here is a delineation of a few historical considerations which seem to the author to have influenced the role of education in prisoners' regimes over the last two hundred or so years. Nor is the delineation complete. It reflects the author's research interests, his solicitude for Robert Raikes in a book dedicated to his commemoration, and his loyalty to the editor's requirements. Others may prefer a different historical context: as research slowly proceeds in this undeservedly neglected field of our social history, there will no doubt be room for alternative approaches. That the author dwells at length on the historical context reflects his view that nothing is explicable about Prison Service establishments or, more generally, the Home Office, except in the perspective of time. That he also sees education not so much in its own right but as part of prisoners' regimes in the round takes account of his further view that no aspect of prison treatment is explicable except in terms of prison treatment overall. Finally, the chapter concludes with one or two speculations on future arrangements for prisoners' education. Space does not admit, unfortunately, of an in-depth analysis of the many fascinating issues which arise.[1]

---

* The author is indebted to the Home Office for permission to consult papers which are not normally available to the public. He, not the Home Office, is responsible for the facts stated and the opinions expressed in this chapter. See also note on p. 166.

The Contemporary Scene[2]

There are currently over a hundred Prison Service establishments in England and Wales accommodating, often in overcrowded and antiquated buildings, some aspects of which,[3] one suspects, would distress John Howard if he were to perambulate them again, an average daily population of 44,000 or so people, including something like 1,500 women and girls. Their educational needs are met by 49 local education authorities employing for the purpose 118 full-time education officers, 263 full-time teachers and 2,818 part-time day and evening teachers. All education staff are employed under the Authorities' usual contracts of service for teachers and salaries are paid in accordance with the Burnham F. E. Salary Reports or whatever hourly rates locally apply in relation to the level of teaching required. Full-time staff are usually attached to colleges of further education or to institutes of adult education for professional support and may as well in some cases be engaged in teaching in them.

The Home Office, which is responsible for custodial establishments through its Prison Department, is statutorily[4] obliged to afford access to educational facilities to people whom they detain on a compulsory, full-time basis if they are of compulsory school age, on a compulsory part-time basis, if they are aged over 16 and under 21 years, and on a voluntary basis if they are aged over 21. On a voluntary basis something like 45 per cent of all adult prisoners participate in educational activities. In individual training prisons the percentage is often higher, sometimes as high as 65 to 70 per cent; but in local prisons, where the physical facilities are often inadequate and the operational pressures very acute, the percentage can be lower than 20. These arrangements have gradually evolved since 1948,[5] when the 1944 Education Act was amended to enable local education authorities to provide teaching staff for education in Prison Service establishments; and since 1953, when the Home Office accepted responsibility for paying the authorities in full for their services from funds voted by Parliament for the treatment and training of people in custody, in place of the rates supplemented by a percentage contribution from the then Ministry of Education towards their general public further education provision which had funded the arrangements since 1948. The Home Office, additionally, is statutorily required to ensure that prisoners are securely and humanely contained when they are remanded in custody by the courts and for the duration of whatever custodial sentences the courts impose on them. Within this duty, further, it is statutorily required actively to promote their physical and mental well-being by every means at its disposal; within the resources of staff, buildings, equipment, and finance available; and within the inherent and unavoidable constraints of custody which, on occasion, may restrict the range of activities available or the manner of their presentation.[6]

Vocational training is provided by qualified Home Office staff. Libraries are provided by the Local Public Library authorities, at Home Office expense. The task of education is very much what it is in the community generally. Thus it is called upon to develop the skills of communication, especially literacy, a most necessary feature of prison education programmes, bearing in mind that something like 8 per cent of all people in Prison Service establishments are illiterate, a percentage which rises to 22 in terms of poor readers, people, say, with a reading age of 10 years.[7] It supports vocational training and employment; enhances personal development through general and higher education; and facilitates recreational and leisure-time pursuits. Literacy is everywhere a part-time day activity, vocational training a full-time one. Recreational education is everywhere a part-time evening activity. General and higher education tend to be split between the day and the evening, in most establishments on a part-time basis by evening, although, in some, especially although not exclusively for young offenders, on a part-time or full-time one by day. In the course of fulfilling these particular tasks, inseparable from any education service at any time nowadays, education makes an important contribution to the quality of life in Prison Service establishments and by occupying prisoners and trainees in ways which require them to exercise self-discipline[8] becomes as important a factor in their management as the supervision of the custodial staff. There is no evidence that education or indeed any other activity practised amongst people in custody, still less the custodial experience itself, is in itself or its immediate effects a cure for crime.[9] But, to the extent that any activity amongst people in custody can be said to widen their horizons or lead to the discovery of the full self, or provide material for reflection, or put people in the way of knowledge and skill through learning experiences, all matters valuable in themselves, then education, which is rich in all these attributes, clearly helps people to live healthily through the tunnel of time which is their sentence, influences their attitudes and relationships and may assist them to resettle into the community when the time comes. As to what they do with their lives after their release, that, of course, is their business and in our community their privilege. A prisoner caught the ethos of a good custodial education service very well when he remarked of his own:

> No matter what I do, I shall always remember that course. The Assistant Governor was keen and he got about 6 of us to go. I was afraid to say anything at first, but the tutor made us write out little pieces to read – we discussed everything from poems to capital punishment – and it was good to disagree with someone without being put on report. We came to read a lot and think a lot. 'Charismatic' is the word I'd use – though I didn't know it then. Whatever I do, I'll always look back on those Tuesdays. We were free for 2 hours every Tuesday – it kept me going and has done ever since.[10]

In those words, although he probably did not know it, he has provided one of the best definitions of adult education in prison there could possibly be.

Historical Context: The Long Haul[11]

(a) *Robert Peel's Gaol Act 1823*

Prison schoolmasters statutorily originated in Robert Peel's Gaol Act 1823.

> Provision shall be made in all Prisons for the Instruction of Prisoners of both Sexes in Reading and Writing, and that Instruction shall be afforded under such Rules and Regulations, and to such Extent, and to such Prisoners, as to the Visiting Justices may seem expedient.[12]

Schoolmasters had not featured in earlier prison legislation and to this day the precise circumstances which occasioned their inclusion in Peel's Act still await full explanation. Their inclusion is usually attributed[13] to the influence of Elizabeth Fry[14] whose activities amongst prisoners in Newgate Gaol, begun some years previously, had gradually attracted widespread public attention. Useful work in association was practised amongst the women and children in custody, knitting stockings for the Foundlings Institute and making clothes for the poor. Basic literacy and numeracy were inculcated on the monitorial system and religious teaching was an essential ingredient of their regime. Mrs Fry was not the only operator of this kind in prisons as the contemporary activities of Sarah Martin[15] in Yarmouth Gaol abundantly testify although, lacking Mrs Fry's social connections, her work was less well known. Here and there, about the same time, may also be found one or two examples of education being regularly practised amongst children and young people in prison, more after 1800, however, than before.[16] Thus, whilst instances can be quoted[17] from the sixteenth century onwards of literate prisoners occasionally helping their illiterate brethren to prepare their cases for presentation to the courts, of prisoners sometimes reading and discussing their literature with each other and of a few prisoners engaging in literary composition, Sir Walter Raleigh and John Bunyan[18] amongst them, to say nothing of a short-lived school in Newgate Gaol during the eighteenth century and the occasional Sunday school towards the end of the century, in which the hand of Robert Raikes[19] may be discerned, there is really nothing about any of these occurrences to suggest education in the sense of continuous, regular, organized teaching and learning. That came later, following the passage of Peel's Act, at first only in the gaols to which the Act applied and then only gradually, very largely at the discretion of Visiting Magistrates. It was a slow process. Even in 1878, 55 years later, when Central Government in the guise of the Prison Commission took over the administration of the country's prisons from the local authorities, there were still only fifty schoolmasters[20] practising in them.

(b) Antecedents

The idea that prisoners should be usefully occupied during their imprisonment, whether in education or other activities, was a late starter in prison history. One explanation lay in the persistence until well into the nineteenth century of a traditional concept of imprisonment associated with remand and short-term confinement. Given until that time the prevalence of transportation and death as common penal sanctions, there was little apparent need for imprisonment as a sanction of real significance in its own right and therefore of measures to occupy prisoners usefully in confinement which are unavoidable once confinement as such, especially lengthy confinement, becomes a major sanction. Transportation was not finally abandoned until after the passing of the Penal Servitude Acts of 1853 and 1857, but it slowly began to wither from the late eighteenth century onwards, following the loss of the American colonies, the interruptions to which it was subjected in the French Revolutionary and Napoleonic Wars and the unwillingness of British overseas territories as they approached internal self-government to continue acting as disposal areas for the mother country's unwanted subjects. The same period also witnessed growing public distaste for widespread and indiscriminate use of the death penalty. Progressive restriction on its application ensured that by the second quarter of the nineteenth century it had been confined solely to murder and treason. This particular development took place in a context of reform in criminal procedure involving greater protection for the accused; of law reform more generally, and of the establishment of a professional police force, all of which contributed to new thought and practice about public law and order. Imprisonment, in short, as a major penal sanction, gradually evolved as an alternative to transportation and the death penalty.

The scene was legislatively set by the Penitentiary Act 1779, and with it for one of the principal disturbances of the public conscience from that day to this, namely how people should be managed, occupied, and generally treated when serving custodial sentences, especially long ones. John Howard, whose *State of the Prisons* appeared in 1777,[21] and his immediate disciples focused public attention on the need to reform prisons physically and to reorganize their internal administration. They advocated secure buildings, designed for this purpose, to facilitate discipline and control and to obviate the need for manacling and other bodily restraints. They stressed the need for buildings which were well ventilated, dry, satisfactorily heated and, above all, clean and sanitary, in place of dark, damp, filthy, disease-ridden premises which were all too frequent at the time. They recommended clean clothing and bedding and regular wholesome food and water for prisoners, forbidding them strong drink and opportunities to mix freely with each other by sex, age, and offence, a practice which bred vice, immorality, and criminal contamination, and gave eighteenth-century prisons their reputation for debased jollity in circumstances of indescribable chaos and squalor. To achieve these reforms, Howard and his disciples laid considerable stress on the employment of salaried staff, carefully selected for their suitability and closely supervised, in place of staff who all too often had no particular fitness for their tasks and were in their employment solely for what they could pecuniarily make out of the prisoners by subjecting them to all manner of fees and practising on them every kind of abuse. They and those whom they influenced, however, were not in business to gratify prisoners. They recognized that prisoners are human beings and for that reason must be treated in a civilized manner, but, as prisoners, they had offended their fellow men and women and for the duration of their sentences they must therefore be punished. Their recommended method was to subject them to a rigorous regime of deterrence and reformation experienced in hard labour, religious instruction, and a measure of solitary confinement, or, as the Penitentiary Act 1779 solemnly expressed it:

> ... if many Offenders, convicted of Crimes for which Transportation hath been usually inflicted, were ordered to solitary Imprisonment, accompanied by well regulated Labour, and Religious Instruction, it might be The Means, under Providence, not only of deterring others from the Commission of the like Crimes, but also of reforming the Individuals, and inuring them to Habits of Industry; . . .[22]

(c) *Local Authority Initiatives: Gloucestershire and Robert Raikes*[23]

The Act influenced the rebuilding of a number of gaols and houses of correction by a few prison authorities up and down the country between that time and the early years of the nineteenth century, amongst them the Gloucestershire magistrates under the dynamic leadership of Sir George Paul, the most thorough-going of all Howard's immediate disciples. Robert Raikes, an admirer of Howard whom he once entertained in his home and who was associated with Paul's rebuilding scheme, had already long campaigned in his newspaper for the reform of the country's iniquitous prisons. Prison reform was nothing new: it dated from the end of the seventeenth century. The plight of debtors, especially if they came from decent, law-abiding families, or crises in public health associated with gaol fever highlighted the need from time to time. The approach tended to be philanthropic, in the mainstream of that growing humanitarian movement[24] which had done so much over the years to transform man's attitude towards man and is with us today in what is sometimes described as 'the caring society'. As the eighteenth century advanced and turned into the nineteenth the movement increasingly became impregnated with the teachings of evangelical religion and utilitarian philosophy, especially as that philosophy was expounded by Jeremy Bentham both in its application to law reform and to prison administration. Bentham, indeed, devoted a large part of his life to devising a model prison, a 'panopticon' as he called it, and tried in vain to persuade successive governments to build it. Commentators on Bentham have tended to see it as a great man's quirk but it may have had a closer bearing on his philosophy than has all too often hitherto been allowed.[25] Be that as it may, Raikes approached prison reform from philanthropic, humanitarian, and evangelical angles. He believed that ignorance begat 'habits of vice and profanity' which in their turn led to crime and penal sanctions. He was particularly appalled by the physical conditions of imprisonment which in his view served only to stimulate the very factors he considered most led to criminal behaviour and the need for measures to contain it. He was well known for his many personal acts of charity and kindness towards individual prisoners who came to his notice, but, as time went by, he came round to the view that action of this nature was not by itself enough. After he became acquainted with the work of Howard, for example, he began to lay stress on the need to make convicted prisoners take part in regular employment. He was, indeed, by no means unaware of the effects of unemployment on behaviour. Unemployment to him was idleness and idleness was connected with drink, gambling, and immoral conduct, 'the corruption of human nature' as he once expressed it, all of which were just as likely to lead to crime as ignorance. Work for some prisoners, especially if coupled with a measure of solitary confinement, might in his view be a more effective deterrent than mere imprisonment as he knew it, but the prison experience should also be used to reform prisoners' personal characters. Work had a part to play in this, too, especially if its content were positive rather than negative, but for true reformation he placed his real faith in education and religious and moral teaching, with education in the role of handmaiden. 'If among the prisoners', it was said, 'he found one who was able to read he gladly made use of him to instruct his fellow prisoners. Some of the younger offenders attained to a competent efficiency in reading.' Raikes is remembered nowadays as the promoter of the Sunday-school movement if not the actual founder of Sunday schools: his work amongst prisoners tends to be over-looked, but it was from his experience of imprisonment as he knew it that he concluded that action was needed to prevent criminals being made in the first place. Sunday schools were conceived by him as fulfilling this requirement quite as much as contributing to people's general well-being and their recognition of their place in the social order of the day. His own Sunday schools functioned on weekdays as well. Learning to read in small classes, the older and more advanced pupils teaching the younger on a sort of monitorial system, in order to master the Bible and appreciate Christian teachings, were their *raison d'être*. Sunday schools do not seem to have proliferated in prisons as they did in the country at large, but, from the closing years of the eighteenth century, examples of them may be found here and there.[26]

(d) *Education Arrangements, 1823–78*

Peel's Act did not introduce anything new into prison treatment as it was then slowly beginning to develop. What it did was to cancel or amend and bring up to date centuries of confused, *ad hoc* legislation and provide local prison authorities to which it applied with clear guidance on how to operate their establishments in future. Guidance was based on the best procedures of the day as they had derived from John Howard and his disciples, from prison reformers more generally, and from the experiences and experiments of the few authorities like Gloucestershire which had endeavoured to carry their recommendations into practice. Separate confinement for men and women, classification, hard useful labour, religious and moral instruction by chaplains, tuition in reading and writing by schoolmasters, a share for prisoners in the profits of their earnings and money to enable them to return home after their discharge were among the many progressive measures recommended. Deterrence, in other words, was harnessed with reformation. Considering the circumstances of the time, it was a remarkable recipe for prison treatment. Unfortunately it has been little studied but it really deserves most careful consideration both in its own right and because of its bearing on today's prison treatment which substantially encapsulates it. The recipe has probably not been studied because in the event the enlightenment and promise of Peel's Act was shortly afterwards extinguished in a welter of imprisonment conceived almost wholly as deterrence, a panic reaction on the part of a public obsessed by a rising crime rate, which ever afterwards has tended to monopolize the attention of commentators. It never really had a chance to prove itself. Only since the Gladstone Committee's condemnation of exclusively deterrent imprisonment at the end of the last century have ways of utilizing the prison experiences more positively begun to appear and they have done so very much in the mirror of Peel's Act. It is significant perhaps that this trend also coincides nowadays with a revival of interest in Bentham, utilitarian philosophy, and classical criminology. The nation, in other words, is moving forward in prison treatment by travelling backwards, surely a unique paradox. Progress since the beginning of this century, however, has been and remains painfully slow. The objectives of the early reformers in their physical and administrative aspects have long been attained, but in their human aspects they still tend to be as elusive as ever. Nevertheless they are there, as the periodic inspiration of individual Prison Service staff such as Alexander Paterson[27] in the 1930s and a host of others before and since has made clear. A major effort of public will expressed in increased resources for the Prison Service is required to capture them and they will then have to be practised in a thorough-going manner before they can be properly evaluated.[28] The rising prison population is not helpful but it is encouraging that nowadays there is a determined search for alternatives to imprisonment as a penal sanction as strong as the one which at the end of the eighteenth and the beginning of the nineteenth centuries looked for alternatives to transportation and the death penalty. It is as if the wheel of imprisonment has turned full circle just as transportation and the death penalty did almost two hundred years ago.

Reverting, however, to the period between 1823 and the advent of the Prison Commission in 1878, prison schoolmasters in alliance with prison chaplains seem to have held their own, certainly in some establishments, despite the eclipse of the enlightenment and promise of Peel's Act. Local authority records are now beginning to reveal a harvest of testament to their activities.[29] Schoolmasters and schoolmistresses, for example, were appointed under the auspices of visiting magistrates and paid out of the local rates. They provided tuition in simple reading and writing for prisoners and trainees most in need, enabling them to study the Bible and profit from the religious and moral instruction of chaplains. Some incorporated number work into their tuition and here and there examples may be found of a wider curriculum redolent of the education and teaching techniques practised in the National Schools of the day. Little is known about their social background, training, if any, and place in the prison hierarchy, but, in time, patient research in a myriad of local archives will no doubt uncover more about them and their work.

(e) The Prison Commission, 1878–1948

The establishment of the Prison Commission in 1878 put a new complexion on their activities. The Act of Parliament which created the Commission[30] nationalized the prisons, expunging the age-old responsibility of the local authorities for their administration, and vested their management in one central unit of administration, capable of acting directly on each prison and standardizing prison treatment everywhere in a way which had not been possible under the local authorities, despite increasing promptings to that end by Home Office prison inspectors since 1835. The Act seems to have cut prison schoolmasters off from their contacts, such as they were, in the community, for thereafter prison treatment of all kinds generally became inward looking, certainly until the Gladstone Committee started to blow away the cobwebs at the end of the century. In some ways the history of prison education from 1878 to 1948, when it became a local responsibility again, may be regarded as a search for the most suitable way back into mainstream education in the community. Prior to the 1920s,[31] the accent was very much on a strict version of the 3 Rs with considerable limitations on prisoners who might benefit from them. There was, however, a movement away from reading and writing as the handmaid of Bible reading and chaplains' religious and moral teachings, a movement which reflected the importance of these skills in their own right, something which everyone needed to cope efficiently with life and work in an increasingly complex and technical society. It also reflected a certain measure of disillusion with the sort of through-going religious and moral teaching which had been regarded as counteracting crime and had characterized much prison treatment in the earlier years of the century. Chaplains, in fact, were gradually coming to see their role as being more akin to that of clergymen in society at large. An internal inquiry into prisoners' education and moral instruction led in 1898 to Rules for prison education although in the event and allowing for later amendments they seem to have made little difference to what was actually done. Education remained largely synonymous with the 3 Rs and was school-orientated, but early in the present century, under Winston Churchill's Home Secretaryship, prisoners' library facilities began to improve and lectures and concerts were increasingly introduced into establishments. These developments reflect the interest of Churchill in the work of the Prison Commission and may well have been stimulated by his own experiences as a prisoner in the Boer War.[32]

The Commission's education policies and practices were witheringly attacked by Stephen Hobhouse and Fenner Brockway in their book *English Prisons Today*, published in 1922, based on the Prison System Enquiry Committee set up by the Labour Party's Research Bureau in 1919. They pleaded for easier access to such education facilities as existed, for an adult rather than a school approach, for facilities for prisoners with higher standards of education, for art and craft activities, and for independent inspection and more competent schoolmasters. The Commission's response was gradually worked out in the 1920s and 1930s. It took the form of basing the curriculum upon the evening institutes of the day and, in the absence of funds, of using voluntary teachers from the community to implement the teaching, the enterprise at each prison being coordinated by the governor advised by an educator of standing in the neighbourhood.[33] Thus such subjects as drama, debates, literature, languages, humanities more generally, music, arts, and handicrafts found their way into prison education programmes outside working hours and have remained there ever since. In the process there was unlocked that wider view of imprisonment as an instrument for the positive training of those subjected to it, an approach favoured by prison reformers in the eighteenth and early nineteenth centuries and in the 1920s and 1930s particularly associated with Alexander Paterson[34] and other colleagues in the then Prison Service. The Prison Commission at that time also developed the helpful habit of seeking the advice of H.M. Inspectors of Schools, particularly about arrangements for young offenders' education, and by 1939 was actually in correspondence with the Treasury about the appointment of its own professional chief education officer. And it was during these inter-war years that the role of chaplains in prisoners' education began to contract. There were misgivings into which William Temple, then Archbishop of York, found himself drawn, but he seems to have come round to the view in the end that the new arrangements would benefit education and enable chaplains to concentrate on the development of their more spiritual and religious duties.[35] All these promising developments were cut short by the outbreak of the Second World War which, however, contributed vocational training to prisoners' regimes through the skilled industrial training which certain prisoners received in Maidstone and Wakefield prisons as part of the Prison Commission's contribution to the war effort preparatory to their being discharged into factory work. From the time of the Gladstone Committee and especially between the two World Wars the search was clearly on in the Prison Commission for a means whereby education in prisoners' regimes could be brought into touch again with mainstream, professional education in the community, from which the Act creating the Commission had severed it.

When they began to consider their post-war arrangements for prisoners' education, therefore, the Commissioners had to hand more than a century's experience of custodial education. It embodied the 3 Rs, especially literacy; libraries, lectures, and concerts; liberal education of the evening institute type; embryonic skilled industrial training; and their immediate pre-war plan for an education department of their own headed by a professional educator and administrator. The experience reflected the humanitarian and reformist philosophies of the late eighteenth and early nineteenth centuries, clear at last of the avowedly punitive and deprivatory practices which had so long engulfed them.

The Age of the Local Education Authorities
1948 to Date[36]

The immediate background to the contemporary scene in prisoners' education with which this chapter began has now to be stated. Following the war, the Prison Commission appointed an advisory committee to recommend future arrangements. Its principal recommendation was that such arrangements should be entrusted to the local education authorities, one of which, Durham, had recently run a successful experiment in voluntary evening-institute education in Durham Prison. Education for young and adult offenders alike was conceived in part-time terms in much the same way as it was for people in the community who were over the school-leaving age and in employment. The most convenient time of day for it in prisons as in the community was considered to be the evening, although facilities for young offenders in need of literacy tuition were made available to them in the day. Teachers served on a part-time basis including those responsible for the overall organization in each prison, part-time principals or tutor-organizers (now Education Officers) as they were at first called. They gradually took over everywhere the last remaining responsibilities of chaplains for education, increasingly so whenever they began to serve on a full-time basis. With the advent of detention-centre training in 1948, for example, persons of compulsory school age had to be catered for and this made necessary the engagement of full-time teaching staff and full-time education programmes. But a full-time education staff presence was slow to develop. It depended on the scale and variety of education available in each establishment which in its turn depended on funds to pay local education authorities for their services, the availability of education accommodation, internal prison management structures, and the priority then given to manual labour in prisoners' regimes. Education programmes developed more extensively among young offenders than adult offenders; this was hardly surprising in view of their age and the borstal-training ethic; but, for the reasons indicated, it was not until the early 'seventies generally that most organizational staff had become full-time and a build-up of full-time teachers commenced. The Commission's first professional Chief Education Officer who was appointed to inaugurate the new arrangements died after only a few years in office and was not replaced. Instead, the Commission managed prisoners' education through an Assistant Commissioner who also had other duties of a non-educational nature to perform. Professionally he was guided by H.M. Inspectorate of Schools which from time to time fully inspected the new education arrangements everywhere. Their partnership had many achievements to its credit, engineered in circumstances of great financial and managerial difficulty in both the Commission's headquarters and individual Prison Service establishments. Its great weakness lay in the absence of a regular flow of on-going advice, information and guidance to establishments and their supporting Local Education Authorities. Moreover, the part-time nature of the organizational staff made it impossible for them to attend properly to their administration, or take part in casework with prisoners, or participate in institutional management meetings because they were present for the most part at times of day when Governors and other

Prison Service staff were not normally on duty. Accommodation, moreover, in too many institutions, especially for adult offenders, was thoroughly unsatisfactory, unattractive to prisoners and teachers alike. The momentum, such as it was, was weakened in the 'sixties by the retirement of Sir Lionel Fox, Chairman of the Prison Commission, who had inspired and vigorously supported the new arrangements from the start, by the retirement of the principal member of H.M. Inspectorate of Schools concerned, and the diversion of the Assistant Commissioner to other duties. These developments coincided with a major rise in the prison population and the advent of more dangerous prisoners, both of which focused greater attention on security, placed it under greater strain, and led to a major inquiry by Lord Mountbatten into prison escapes. The review of prison administration, institutional and Headquarters management, finance and regimes which his Report brought about was largely instrumental in enabling arrangements for prisoners' education to be put on a more suitable professional and organiza-tional footing. To quote but a few examples: the accent on a full-time institutional presence; the development of regional Prison Service staff; closer relationships with individual local education authorities, the Local Authorities' and Teachers' Associations nationally, the Universities, H.M. Inspectorate of Schools and the Departments of Employment and of Education and Science, leading to the formulation of general policy and practice; the unification of education, vocational training, and library provision into one further education service in place of the former three separate services; improving accommodation and equipment; better in-service train-ing for education staff; and a growing realization of prisoners' needs which education services can help to meet, with an increasing share in prisoners' day regimes which this presupposes. Education arrangements in Prison Service establishments nowadays still have a long way to go (the cuts in public finance of recent years have not helped) before they can meet all the needs and overcome all the difficulties confronting them, but after two hundred years they have at last come of age and are well poised for a further breakthrough as recommended at the end of 1979 in the Report of the May Committee.

The Future

The future for education services amongst adult prisoners is likely to be in the expansion of present-day literacy education into day numeracy and day social education, good all-round adult basic education, along lines which have already been pioneered in a number of establishments; and closer links everywhere, in the interests of both young and adult offenders, with the Department of Employment and Local Education Authorities over careers guidance, job-training, and job-selection. There is a good likelihood that imaginative developments which are currently taking place to improve prisoners' libraries in association with the Public Library Authorities will be fully realized. There may not be all that of a future for more full-time education facilities amongst adult prisoners, outside widely ranging adult basic education, but there is clearly one for selected trainees in young offender establishments and a very good one for more intra-mural, part-time, day and block release opportunities in both these and adult offender establishments. All the indications are that in due course new sentences will take the place of the present separate borstal, detention, and young prisoner sentences for young offenders and that this will make possible a major review of the provision for their education.[37] Vocational training, especially among young offenders, will modify its character to take account of the job-training policies now being pioneered by the Department of Employment and the D.E.S., particularly amongst unemployed and often educationally disadvantaged school-leavers. There is scope for increased co-operation with the Prison Department's Directorate of Industries and Farms in areas of skills training within the regime. More consultative management within education centres and a more consultative style as between education centres and their prisoner and trainee clients, however, are required to bring about these developments, as also a resumption of the prison building programme to replace the remaining unsuitable education accommodation. Local provision is the characteristic of prison education and this is valuable bearing in mind that in other respects anyway no two Prison Service establishments are alike, but it makes for a certain unevenness of provision and administration. Here and there the diversity is too wide and this needs to be remedied. Fortunately the local education authorities are taking their providing duties more seriously than before, and in each establishment fostering its relationship with its particular authority there lies the possibility of a considerable improvement everywhere in administrative and professional know-how and a handsome pay-off in staff in-service training and in careers-guidance and counselling for staff. In this particular matter, there is much to be said for establishing a suitably constituted consultative committee on prison education incorporating all the current *ad hoc* forums for the discussion and monitoring of educational policy and practice, to match the Joint Negotiating Committee[38] for salaries and conditions of service and the Committee under consideration to further prison library developments. But, of course, it will all take time. Gears will clash. Issues will have to be worked through. Success will depend on everyone concerned putting first what matters, encouraging prisoners to use the education and training facilities provided. That is where dedication comes in. It is, one suspects, the dedication and only the dedication of education, vocational training, and other associated staff which has kept prison education going since its regular inception in 1823. These are the characteristics which will be required of all concerned in the times of change which lie ahead. There is a need for patience, to work through established and well-tested channels and to look for results over periods of five to ten years rather than tomorrow or a year or two on. And it is necessary to be realistic, to appreciate that, amid the human mess which characterizes imprisonment, the opportunities for enlargement are limited. But let heart be taken from the very great deal that can be done and is in fact done. There is now a widespread recognition that imprisonment is on too big a scale and that the Prison Department might be able to do a better job on a more intensive basis with a smaller population, a situation crying out for realization. Meanwhile, education staff must carry on as best possible; knowing that the system needs them; that it would be infinitely worse without them; and that the main criticism prisoners and trainees make of them is in fact their tribute to them, that there are not enough of them. Their predecessors have provided them with their foundations. Let us hope that the structure now being raised on those foundations will be worthy of them in every way and of their present-day successors.

NOTES

1 This will be attempted in a forthcoming publication of the National Institute of Adult Education which will be devoted to the practice of adult education amongst people detained in today's Prison Service establishments.

2 Facts and figures to illustrate this section of the chapter, which incorporates memorabilia personal to the author, will be found in the Annual Reports of the Prison Department, 1967 to date, and in *Prisons and the Prisoner*, 1977, both published by H.M.S.O. Pages 36 to 40 of the latter deal with education, libraries, and vocational training, but the whole publication is a useful guide to the philosophy and practice of present day imprisonment in England and Wales. J. E. Hall Williams, *Changing Prisons*, Peter Owen Limited, 1975, may also be consulted.

3 Overcrowding, for example. Annual Report of the Prison Department, 1977, paras 65, 102, 105, and 112. Also the 1979 Report.

4 Statutory Instruments 1952 No. 1432, 1964 No. 388, 1964 No. 387.

5 Education (Miscellaneous Provisions) Act 1948.

6 Notably where science subjects involving laboratory work are concerned, especially the use of chemicals. Not all 'kit-requiring' subjects, however, are necessarily ruled out.

7 On literacy, see, in addition to the information contained in the Annual Reports of the Prison Department, the three Annual Reports of the Adult Literacy Resources Agency Management Committee, 1976, 1977, and 1978, chapters on penal establishments, H.M.S.O.

8 What is important here, especially amongst prisoners serving long sentences, is the tonic properties of education. Educators always have to be on the alert lest education should be practised consciously or unconsciously as an opiate, i.e. simply as a means to keep people quiet. This is an ever-present danger of any activity of any kind practised amongst people in long-term custody especially of a high security nature. Vigilance is essential.

9 Hence the current spate of attacks on imprisonment as a penal sanction, fortified by dismay at its rising financial cost, i.e. £219,853m total net expenditure in 1976–77. Within this figure, net current expenditure totalled £183,630m. The annual average cost of a person in custody was £4,420. The Annual Report of the Prison Department, 1977, H.M.S.O., para. 24 and Appendix No. 4. The argument for more alternatives to imprisonment cannot be gainsaid, yet the case for imprisoning certain kinds of offenders remains strong; but, so long as the community remains wedded to imprisonment as a penal sanction, if only for fewer people, the problem will remain of what to do with them during their custody, especially people who are serving long sentences. The fact that all but an infinitesimal minority of them will return to the community one day where, hopefully, they will then live at peace with their fellow men and women, and considerations of humanity alike suggest to many people that there should be a variety of occupations for them in custody of a kind which will help them to survive

in good mental and physical health throughout their imprisonment and to manage themselves satisfactorily after their release.

10 W. Forster, *The Higher Education of Prisoners*, Vaughan Paper No. 21, Department of Adult Education, Leicester University, p. 19.

11 There is a vast literature about imprisonment in the round, but not a great deal that is really all that significant about the practice of education amongst people in custody. Among the works which may be consulted, by way of general background to this chapter, the author has found the following few generally useful:

L. Radzinowicz, *A History of English Criminal Law*, vol. i, London, 1948.

S. and B. Webb, *English Prisons Under Local Government*, London, 1922.

U. R. Q. Henriques, 'The Rise and Decline Of the Separate System Of Prison Discipline', *Past and Present*, no. 54, February, 1972. (A valuable up-dating and reconsideration of some of S. and B. Webb, op. cit., whose classic account is now in need of revision as a whole.)

Sir Lionel Fox, *The English Prison and Borstal Systems*, London, Routledge and Kegan Paul, 1952.

J. E. Hall Williams, op. cit.

D. L. Howard, *The Education Of Offenders*, Bibliographic Series No. 5, University of Cambridge, Institute of Criminology, Cambridge, 1971.

Other works are mentioned in the footnotes, below. The works cited in this chapter are not intended to be exhaustive but simply a first guide to what is generally available.

12 Clause X, sub-clause 10, 4 Geo. IV, Cap. LXIV. Pickering's Statutes, p. 484.
Clause XXVI provided for the payment of schoolmasters and others out of the rates.

13 S. and B. Webb, op. cit., certainly thought so and for the time being their explanation still stands.

14 J. Witney, *Elizabeth Fry*. Harrap, Guild Books, 1937. John Kent, *Elizabeth Fry*. Batsford, 1962.

15 A useful account of her work may be found in Frances Banks, *Teach Them To Live*, London, Max Parish, 1958. *Howard Journal*, vol. vii, contains an article about her by M. F. Lloyd-Pritchard, 1948–49.

16 Author's own researches.

17 J. S. Cockburn, ed., *Crime In England, 1550 to 1800*, Methuen, 1977, ch. 10, is interesting to consult.

18 E. Stockdale, *A Study of Bedford Prison, 1660 to 1877*. Phillimore, 1977.

19 See n. 23, below.

20 S. and B. Webb, op. cit.

21 See also *Prisons Past and Future*, ed. for the Howard League of Penal Reform by J. C. Freeman, London, Heinemann, 1978, a bicentennial commemoration of Howard's book. There is an interesting critique of Howard in *History*, vol. lxii, no. 206, October 1977, by Rod Morgan, who rightly points out that Howard's concept of prison as a fraternally adminis-

tered and well regulated community in which everyone knew his place and was expected to keep it had much in common with other social engineering of the day, exemplified by 'Howard's own estate at Cardington, Arkwright's mill at Cromford, Wedgwood's Etruria, Raikes's Sunday Schools, Hanway's Marine Society.' Mrs Fry's education schemes and Peel's Act were a faithful mirror of such engineering, a circumstance which helps to explain why they attracted so large a measure of acceptance, although not necessarily always a complete one.

22   Clause V, Geo. III, 1779, C. 74, Cap. LXXIV, Pickering's Statutes, p. 419.

23   J. R. S. Whiting, *Prison Reform In Gloucestershire 1776 to 1820*, Phillimore, 1975; H. P. R. Finberg, ed., *Gloucestershire Studies*, Leicester University Press, 1957, chapter on Sir George Onesiphorus Paul by E. A. L. Moir; A. Gregory, *Robert Raikes*, Hodder and Stoughton, 1877. Guy Kendall, *Robert Raikes*, Nicholson and Watson, 1939, from which the quotations in this chapter are extracted.

24   As evidenced, for example, in the foundation of hospitals and infirmaries, in the charity school movement, in attempts to reform the Poor Law, in the growing attack on slavery and so on.

25   On Bentham, utilitarian philosophy, and its influence see A. V. Dicey, *Law and Opinion in England during the Nineteenth Century*, Macmillan, first published 1905 and reprinted many times since. It is a classic, but dated nowadays. Gertrude Himelfarb in an essay entitled 'The Haunted House of Jeremy Bentham', which appears in her book *Victorian Minds*, Weidenfeld and Nicholson, 1968, has admirably anatomized the 'panopticon'.

26   Author's researches.

27   S. K. Ruck, ed., *Paterson On Prisons*, London, Frederick Muller, 1951.

28   Early reformers valued imprisonment in terms of the measures of deterrence and rehabilitation embodied in the daily regimes of offenders subjected to them. Much opinion today, however, scouts both measures, especially those concerned with rehabilitation. Instead, measures such as education, physical education, vocational training, industry, farming, and so on are coming to be valued partly for their intrinsic worth, partly as useful mental and physical occupations during imprisonment and partly for their potential to help people when they emerge from custody to integrate themselves into the community. It seems to be a more realistic attitude in today's circumstances and has some bearing on the growing dilemma in the community of how law-abiding members are going to conduct themselves in the era of 'enforced-leisure' unemployment, which is now starting to stare the community in the face. The May Committee shared this view.

29   Author's researches.

30   There is an excellent analysis of this Act by L. J. Blom-Cooper in *Prisons Past And Future*, op. cit.

31   See Annual Reports of the Prison Commission; J. E. Thomas, *The English Prison Officer Since 1850*, Routledge and Kegan Paul, 1972; Du Cane, *Punishment and Prevention of Crime*, 1885; Sir E. Ruggles-Brise, *The English Prison System*, London, Macmillan, 1921.

32 House of Commons Hansard, 20 July 1910, cols. 1349–50. A good Churchill story. The whole speech, however, with its truly moving peroration repays careful study. It is as fresh today as when it was written.

33 C. O. G. Douie, 'The Unresolved Conflict XII: Prison', *Journal of Education*, February 1950.

34 S. K. Ruck, ed., *Paterson On Prisons*, op. cit.
   In this and the concluding section of the chapter there are memorabilia personal to the author.

35 S. K. Ruck, op. cit.

36 See Annual Reports of the Prison Commission leading into those of the Prison Department 1948 to date; Frances Banks, *Teach Them to Live*, op. cit.; *Royal Commission on the Penal System in England and Wales*, vol. i, H.M.S.O., 1967; *People In Prison*, Cmnd. Paper 4214, H.M.S.O., 1969; *Prisons And The Prisoner*, H.M.S.O., 1977; *Report of the Enquiry into Prison Escapes and Security*, Cmnd. 3175, H.M.S.O., 1966; ('The Mountbatten Report'); *The Regime for Long-Term Prisoners in Conditions of Maximum Security* ('The Radzinowicz Report'), 1968; Home Office Prison Department Policy Statements: *Education in Prisons*, 1969; *Treatment of Women and Girls in Custody*, 1970; *Education In Detention Centres*, 1971; *Education in Establishments for Women and Girls*, 1973; *Vocational Training for People in Custody*, 1973; *Library Facilities for People in Custody*, 1978; Report of the Advisory Council on the Penal System, *Detention Centres*, 1970; Report of the Advisory Council on the Penal System, *The Young Adult Offender*, 1974; *A Strategy For The Basic Education Of Adults*, Report to the Advisory Council for Adult and Continuing Education, April 1979.

37 *Youth Custody and Supervision: A New Sentence*, Cmnd. 7406, H.M.S.O., 1978. The advent of a Conservative government following the 1979 general election, however, had modified these proposals, as its White Paper (Cmnd 8045) of October 1980 reveals; but the commitment to education and other measures to enhance the development and maturation of young offenders in custody is stressed.

38 This Committee interprets the application of The Burnham Further Education Salary Reports in relation to prison education. The Consultative Committee is now formally under consideration.

NOTE: At the time of writing, Mr Justice May's Report on the United Kingdom Prison Services had not been published. The Report commends the present arrangements for prisoners' education and recommends their further development.

The Child
in the Urban Industrial Mission

Kathryn Copsey

The Everyday Experience of the Inner City Child

There are four important factors in the experience of the inner city child: (a) environment, (b) materialism, (c) family breakdown, (d) multi-racial context. Although such aspects are also relevant to the experience of the suburban or rural child, it may be argued that in the inner city there are fewer positive forces at work to counteract their influence.

Environment

Favourite tower block game:

First: Smash windows on stairwells.
Then: How far up a tower block do you have to go in order for a full milk bottle to penetrate the roof of the youth centre next door?
Answer: 16 floors.

Growing up in the inner city is very different to growing up in the country or even the suburbs. The average inner city child faces a world of concrete and asphalt, of redevelopment and rehousing schemes, of tower blocks and factories, of education cutbacks and industry removals, of racial disharmony and alienation. Such aspects may, in themselves, be neither good nor bad in the mind of the child, they may not even impinge on his consciousness. They are simply a part of the facts of life. But all of this is the reality of inner city living.

One factor whose importance is often underestimated in the inner city is the lack of adequate play space for children. Whereas in suburban areas a garden is a *sine qua non*, in many homes in the inner city gardens are too small for adequate play or are simply non-existent. Tower blocks have only a patch of grass the size of a pocket handkerchief at their foot if that. This lack of 'private space' is one of the significant disadvantages for the inner city child. He has no area in which to mend his bike or build something which he can then leave in safety to another time. Where council-operated play areas are available, these are often dangerous for small children because of broken glass, or are locked up because vandalism has made the play equipment unsafe. In certain enlightened local authorities, demolition sites are flattened and grassed over to make temporary play spaces. Generally, however, the majority of such sites are boarded up and left to the imagination of youngsters who see a challenge in climbing over the corrugated fencing and playing in the rubble – the more so if it is marked 'keep out'. Consequently, children often tend to play in the only area left available to them – the road – and the possibility of traffic accidents mounts. Voluntary agencies, including churches, who attempt to do something innovative for children, such as a children's house or adventure playground, frequently face opposition from local residents who fear disturbance may result. Gates, windows, doors, and walls are common targets of pointless destruction and vandalism as many youngsters, consciously or unconsciously, vent their frustration on an establishment which they see as militating against them in terms of everything from education to employment.

Although many councils no longer build them, tower blocks abound in many districts, described as 'one way streets going nowhere'. The social problems associated with them are numerous, especially where they are used to house young families. Other families are housed in pre-fabs, built immediately following the war with an anticipated life-span of ten years. Thirty years later they are still occupied. Many redevelopment areas can be found where entire streets of terraced houses are boarded up with the exception of two or three isolated houses. As they await rehousing, the people in these houses are easy prey to vandalism. Old-age pensioners are afraid to stay in their homes alone with no near neighbours, but are afraid to leave the house empty. Still other families have lived many years in unbelievably run-down accommodation, with dampness and rats a very present concern, and with outside toilets and no proper bathroom facilities. Home tensions arise as rooms are overcrowded and privacy and space are virtually non-existent. Children tend to grow up very young in such a context, left to look after younger brothers and sisters when they themselves may be only nine or ten. As immigrants move in, tensions over housing and jobs mount and the newcomers are frequently seen as convenient scapegoats in such situations. Those most socially mobile and financially able move out of the area leaving the elderly, the young marrieds not yet able to afford a new home, the immigrants, and the least socially able.

Many of those who move do so because they are not happy with the quality of the education available for their children. Inner city districts frequently draw teachers on their probationary year or those who cannot find a job in more popular areas. Many of these consequently lack both the necessary experience and the commitment and sense of challenge essential to working with inner city youngsters. There is a high turnover of staff and a succession of supply teachers as many vacancies remain unfilled. Such teacher shortage has clearly taken its toll on the quality of education. A few years ago children in schools in one of London's inner city boroughs faced a $3\frac{1}{2}$-day week for a considerable period. Resources, ranging from new buildings to new books, are scarce. Priority in such matters frequently goes to new towns and suburbs where the quality of education has to keep pace with the growing population. Inner city areas are left with decaying buildings and out-dated resources. Where the availability or quality of a job bears little relation to the nature of the education offered, it is to be expected that the value placed on education and the priority accorded to it would be minimal. Education is a prelude to work rather than a means of opening up new opportunities.

How does the Church respond to children living in such a situation?

Materialism

'How come he gets free school meals and his dad can buy him an £80 skateboard?' – bewildered child to parents.

Deprivation for the child in the inner city is frequently not manifested in economic terms but rather in terms of a lack of adequate love, care, and adult supervision. Although there are still many homes where there is not much money, there are few really poor families. It is interesting to note that many of the families with whom social workers have contact because the children are classified as being 'at risk', are homes which have many modern conveniences: colour television, washing machine, three-piece suite. Yet these are the same families who will bemoan the fact that they have not enough money to buy their own house or move out of the area. The issue here is one of priorities: whereas in some areas a family may choose to save money to buy a house, many families in the inner city prefer to spend and have immediately. Children regularly appear at after-school clubs with 50p or £1 to spend on sweets. Within the West Indian community priority is often given to buying a large car – possibly an American model – or to brightly decorating the exterior of the house.

Growing up in such a context gives a child a sense of the power of money at an early age. Money can procure him all he wants materially speaking. He also has a sense of the immediacy with which this can happen. Even if he has not enough money at a given time, he can buy on hire purchase. There is very little priority placed on the value of delayed rewards; hence, for example, a low value is placed on education. Why stay in school and study when, ultimately, the likelihood of a suitable job being available is small. Peer group pressure in a community where education is relatively unimportant also militates against a youngster staying on at school.

Where money and possessions are available, where schools and youth clubs can frequently boast an abundance of resources, many churches find difficulty in attracting children to their activities having, as they do, to make use of outdated and unsuitable buildings and limited resources.

How does the Church respond to children in such a situation?

Family Breakdown

'Your dad's going out with Kelly and Georgina's mum, isn't he?' – comment by a child in a Sunday school class talk on families.

The pattern of family breakdown has become the norm rather than the exception in many areas, suburban as well as urban. The head teacher of a large London comprehensive estimated that over fifty per cent of his students came from broken homes. Possibly one difference lies in the fact that in suburban areas the tendency is to gloss over the marital breakdown to outsiders whereas in many inner city situations the reality is there for all to see. A teacher in one London Sunday school commented that the majority of his children come from one-parent families. To his knowledge that proportion appeared to be fairly representative of the unchurched families in the area. In many families, the parent that remains with the children has to work. During holiday periods this places a considerable strain on the family as the parent may lose his/her job unless the child can be cared for by a friend or neighbour or in a holiday club. However, it is interesting to note that the children of single-parent families are not necessarily unhappy or poorly adjusted. It is more likely that complete families in which home tensions are the norm are far more detrimental to the psychological and physical well-being of the child. But according to children's workers perhaps some of the greatest emotional tensions for the child are to be found in families of mixed parentage, not in terms of race, but where there are brothers and sisters of several different mothers and fathers within the same family. Here a child has to learn to interact on a family level with other children, possibly near or exactly his own age and with whom he has nothing in common, at virtually a moment's notice. Generally he is not consulted about such a transaction and the sense of insecurity which this can engender in a child is enormous as neither family nor home remains a stable unit.

Many families are further divided by feuds which can be carried on over many generations. A single disagreement can extend to a major confrontation between brother and sister or parents and children, and the tradition of the feud can continue although the original incident may be forgotten. Such feuding can result in fights between the different parties or even murder.

The lack of a stable home also contributes to a high incidence of juvenile crime. Children as young as nine and ten engage in petty theft, breaking and entering, shoplifting, harbouring stolen goods, as well as in acts of vandalism. It is a small step from this to crime on a major scale, stealing cars, robbing shops, even muggings. Where father, brothers, or friends are in and out of prison regularly, children soon accept this pattern of life as normal. Often there is no sense of wrong-doing in the mind of the child. One youngster in a redevelopment area boasted of the new bicycle he was buying. Further questioning established that this was being financed by the copper piping he was removing from derelict houses in the district and selling to a friend of his father's at £20 a bag. He had no thoughts that such an action might be stealing.

How does the Church respond to children in such a situation?

Multi-racial Context

'God is white, like everyone else in this room except me.' – comment by a black child in Sunday school.

Inevitably a consideration of the factors affecting the urban child must take account of the reality of the multi-racial situation now to be found in many inner city districts. Such areas house Indians, Pakistanis, East African Asians, West Indians, Cypriots, and Africans. Inevitably, the ethnic mix leads to considerable tension, not only between the indigenous white population and the new-comers, but also amongst the ethnic communities themselves. Misunderstanding and hostility are unfortunately found as frequently within the Church as outside it and children absorb the prejudices of their parents automatically, often with little understanding as to why they hate the 'wogs and coons'.

In many schools, the multi-ethnic approach has led to religious education becoming a study of comparative religions, of morals, of 'stances for life', as teachers adapt their material to suit the back-grounds of their students. Children are taught the elements of Hinduism, Sikhism, and Islam along with Judaism and Christianity. Assemblies which originally provided the opportunity for the school to worship together, now often function principally as a session for making necessary announcements to the entire school, as otherwise some immigrant families would choose to withdraw their children. In some boroughs the leaders of ethnic groups have approached the local education authority regarding the establishment of separate schools for their children.

Coloured youngsters, caught between the two different cultures of school and home, feel accepted by neither and are often alienated from the only society they have known, since many were born in this country. This conflict is reflected in many practical aspects of life such as friendship, marriage, and work. Within the West Indian community children tend to be brought up under very strict parental control as they are expected to adhere to the pattern of life and culture of the Caribbean. But having grown up in an English society many rebel against this, leaving home as soon as possible. Within the Asian community also the home culture of the child exists in stark contrast to the customs, values, and morals he sees in English society. Many Asian girls are brought up in local schools conforming to English culture but discover upon reaching teenage years that they are forbidden to attend mixed youth clubs. Clubs specifically for Asian girls help to provide recreation for such youngsters. In some situations young girls of marriageable age are transported back to a home country where they face the difficult task of adjusting to a totally new culture. In other situations, girls from overseas are brought to England to marry. They speak no English and find themselves alone and bewildered in a strange land. Their husbands are at work all day and in some instances even forbid their wives to learn the basic English necessary for shopping. Many such women undertake to do home work and find themselves exploited by their employers.

How does the Church respond to children living in such a situation?

Backcloth

General

Having briefly highlighted these four issues, it must be emphasized that inner urban industrialized areas are in no way homogeneous. Even a single inner city borough contains great variation within it and factors applicable to one area may be totally irrelevant to another. Thus in discussing the everyday experience of the inner city child, a generalized situation has been outlined. However, the question remains as to how the Church responds to children living in such a situation, the majority of whom are untouched by any form of Christian mission.

Its response has traditionally manifested itself in a great variety of areas, ranging from aspects of community care – such as playgroups and holiday clubs – through uniformed organizations, to activities with a specific Christian content. Since historically one of the Church's principal methods of reaching children, whatever the denomination, has been the Sunday school, one cannot consider the needs of the urban child in a mission context without assessing the influence of this institution. However, neither should any outreach on the part of the Church amongst children be considered in isolation from the total context of the inner city environment as noted above.

Historical Overview

It is worth bearing in mind that historically, as several authors – notably E. R. Wickham in his analysis of Sheffield – have indicated, the working classes have long been alienated from the Church. Even Charles Booth in his analysis of *The Life and Labour of the People in London* at the beginning of this century distinguished between the various classes of people who attend church.

> The five classes which we have recognized are wealth (with fashion), upper middle class (without fashion), lower middle class, regular wage earners, and the poor . . . The poor can indeed be visited, but they cannot be induced to come to church . . . A smaller church or mission hall must be built. It shall be their own and they will come. But they do not.[1]

Transferring this analysis to a modern context, it is possible to dichotomize between the 'roughs' and the 'respectables' within a working class community along the lines of the differentiation outlined by Josephine Klein.[2] Thus one observes that the incidence of church-going among the 'respectables' – those who, according to census data, fall into the economically skilled or professional category and are private tenants or owner/occupiers – is much greater than amongst the 'roughs'. It is interesting that this distinction may be observed within an inner city community which to the outsider is apparently homogeneous.

From 1740 onwards, the Industrial Revolution caused people to move from the country to the growing towns in search of work. This resulted in the loss of influence of the established Church with its landed interests and 'squarson' (squire-parson) ideal. The rise of evangelical nonconformity, with its emphasis on lay participation, initially counteracted the loneliness of industrial life. The chapel became the focal point in an associational network of religious, social, and recreational services. Originally the Sunday school arose independently of either chapel or church. It was a separate institution designed to provide a release for the child from the long hours and grim factory conditions, and to teach the rudiments of education within a Christian context. However, by 1870 the State had undertaken responsibility for providing a basic education and the Sunday school, which had been independent and non-denominational, increasingly became the agent of individual denominations in recruitment. Socialization of juveniles rather than adult conversion became a major form of recruitment. In terms of numbers, the Sunday school reached its height in the Victorian era, offering numerous related activities to which scholars could belong, such as a

Band of Hope, or a Christian Endeavour Society, as well as recreational and sports clubs. Even today, elderly Sunday school teachers recall with great nostalgia schools of 3–400 children, scarcely comprehending that by present standards 30 to 40 is a good number, while ten or a dozen children is the norm in many schools. This drop in numbers, while undoubtedly characteristic of suburban and rural schools also, is particularly apparent in inner city areas where many Sunday schools have simply dwindled and closed owing to lack of children and shortage of adequate staff.

In general terms, it would appear that the decline in Sunday-school attendance began slowly in the years immediately following World War I. As early as 1916 one London Sunday school convened a conference 'to discuss the falling off of scholars and the relationship of the church and Sunday school'. The decline accelerated in the years following World War II, and in 1961 it was estimated that only five per cent of the total population of England, Scotland, and Wales were enrolled in Sunday school. There is little reason to suppose that this trend has been reversed in the present decade. Indeed, in one London borough in 1978, only 1·4 per cent of the total population of that borough attended Sunday school. This decline has taken place despite the fact that in recent years there has been a plethora of leaflets, pamphlets, and occasional papers published regarding the relationship of the child to the Church; new theories of reaching the children have been expounded; new Sunday-school structures recommended; new methods of building relationships with the parents advocated and numerous training days and workshops have been held. The local Sunday school appears to have remained comparatively unaffected by such theoretical recommendations, and the degree to which the potential for the practical application of such theories has been realized at the local level is to be questioned.

The Contemporary Scene

Have the Church and the traditional Sunday school anything to offer to the contemporary inner city child that he wants and that is attractive to him? The Church has an abundance of answers as to what he needs, but it would do well to recall that both Church and Sunday school are voluntary agencies with a comparatively low attraction and adherence level. Possibly a greater awareness is needed as to what is attractive to the child. It is interesting to observe that in many Sunday schools although the societal context and the function of the school have changed considerably over the past fifty years, often the basic form has altered very little. Thus, while in a contemporary day school setting learning involves the use of all the senses, together with a considerable degree of physical activity, many Sunday schools continue to operate on the basis of the traditional classroom wherein teaching takes the form of input by the teacher to a passive and sedentary group of pupils.

There are several factors, in addition to those noted above, regarding the child in an urban industrialized area with which the Church must be cognizant if it is to develop an effective response to such a child. Thus the typical inner city child:

1. has no Christian home background;
2. has no knowledge or understanding of Jesus (except as a swear word) or the Bible;
3. thinks in concrete, present reality rather than in abstract terms and interests;
4. has grown up at a relatively young age and his experiences and language are frequently far removed from those of his teacher;
5. dismisses or ignores issues which he does not see as directly relevant to him;
6. is often blunt and honest and will not bother to attend Sunday school or any form of Church mission if he does not enjoy it;
7. sees Sunday school or church as an interesting occupation while a child – it is something to do and a place to meet his friends – but generally the Church has no relevance to him and he will probably leave Sunday school when he reaches his early teens.

The Church's Response

The challenge of reaching the unchurched inner city child is enormous, given the traditional failure of the Church in such communities, and the openness, bluntness, warmth, and receptivity of such children to those who are interested in working with them. However, unless new approaches are adopted and new attitudes formed on the part of the Church to children, there continues the grave possibility that the Sunday school in particular, as well as other forms of work with children, may simply serve to inoculate the child further against a continuing involvement in the adult Christian community. It may be argued that in the inner city, the practicalities of methods and materials are of less importance than attitudes and aims in working with children.

To be of maximum effect, the Church needs to focus its thinking on three main issues.

Starting Where the Child Is

It cannot be stressed enough that there is a need to start where the child is rather than where it is thought that he should be. The Church is always very ready to respond to what it thinks a child 'needs', but very often cannot operate at the level of what a child wants or with an approach to which he can respond. Flexibility and adaptability are of paramount importance. So is sensitivity on the part of the worker towards the child as a person in his own right. What does the local newspaper say has been happening in the area? Is the child in a redevelopment zone? Where does he play? What do his parents feel about the Church? Can he read?

Two areas highlight this issue.

1. *Child–Adult Relationships* Often a child has no adult with whom to talk – his parents are at work, at night they are too busy, too tired, watching television, or simply have no interest in taking the time to talk with the children. A child needs an adult to whom he can relate, and a club leader or Sunday school teacher at the church can fulfil this function. It may be that there is greater value for the child in abandoning the prepared material for the day and simply talking, than in pursuing activities merely because they are set. Talking which begins with the concerns and interests of the child is a most effective means of building a relationship.

2. *Christian Education Material* A concern frequently voiced by children's workers and Sunday-school staff in the inner city relates to the nature and content of the bulk of currently available Christian education material which, it is said, does not start with the life experience of the child and does not effectively relate to him. Much of it assumes too great a biblical knowledge and background and draws on situations and illustrations which are totally outside the world of the child in the inner city. Frequently, it is so highly literate and conceptual that even teachers, many of

177

whom lack experience and training, find it difficult to handle and adapt. Publishers concede the need but maintain that it is not financially viable to produce Christian education material specifically for the inner city, neither are there sufficient marketing outlets in such areas. This raises enormous questions which have yet to be adequately answered as to the priorities of the Church towards urban mission.

It is essential that material be grounded in the daily experience of the child. An urban child may enjoy a story about life in the country or the suburbs, but it may be questioned as to whether or not he actually identifies himself with the story presented. Does he make the mental transition from that situation to his own and apply the point of the story to himself? This process, not easy in itself, is further hindered when the child cannot quickly relate to the given situation.

Material also needs to take account of the fact that many youngsters are non-readers, and that the cognitive approach to learning is not necessarily the most effective. Experientially-based learning, in which children are encouraged to learn through the use of all their senses, has been used with great effect amongst urban children.

Finally, those preparing the material must recognize the practicalities of the physical arrangements which face children's workers. Unsuitable buildings, small rooms, crowded rooms in which two or three groups run simultaneously, and lack of easy access to gardens and parks, often make impractical many of the suggestions in the Christian education material. These are not helped by dwindling numbers of children, elderly teachers who find difficulty in keeping pace with modern youth and trends, and young inexperienced teachers who lack any form of training.

Relationships With Parents

The building up of relationships with the parents of children with whom the Church has contact is a much neglected part of urban mission. The reasons for this are numerous. The commuter church syndrome, frequently to be observed in the inner city, means that teachers live outside the area, commuting in simply to attend church and related activities. They do not see either children or parents on a daily basis, and as most formal visiting has to be carried out in the evening, family commitments, transport, or old age often make this impossible. Also, the fact that most parents work means that they are only at home in the evenings, perhaps at weekends, or as their shifts allow them. This not only limits time available for visiting but can also mean that they prefer not to be disturbed in the little free time available to them. A frequent response of children to the question of why their parents do not attend church is that dad is at work. Sunday service times are based on the assumption that parents work a nine-to-five job and a five-day week. They take little account of the fact that shift work is the norm in many families. A building up of relationships with the parents is further hampered in the inner city by the fact that virtually no parents come to church during the year except possibly for one or two major festivals.

In the light of this, one may well ask what is the attitude of the parents towards the Church? Why do they allow or even encourage their children to attend junior church or Sunday school? To some it is a useful babysitter, an occupation for the children for an hour which gets them out of the house. To others, it is a part of the British tradition of growing up: 'I went and it did me no harm so you're going.' To some it is an alternative to the school in terms of religious and moral education. Still others have no interest in the church at all and do not even know where their children are. Children from homes with no church connection are frequently irregular attenders and erratic in their interest.

The myth that unchurched parents can be reached through their children and brought into the Church has largely been dispelled by the realities of the situation. It is doubtful that a church, which has at best only one or two hours with a child in any week and no interaction with the parents, can hope to have any lasting effect on the child.

In view of these factors, and given the importance of building relationships with the parents, a totally new approach is needed. Formal home visiting has increasingly become a less viable proposition. An 'open house' policy is needed instead – literally, a situation in which a Sunday-school teacher or member of a local congregation is known to be free and available for children, parents, and friends to drop in. This is particularly effective where the individuals have children themselves, and a simple act, such as taking a child home, can be a bridge towards building up a relationship. It is essential that such an open house be local to the church. Inner city children, and to a lesser degree adults, tend to be very parochial in their thinking and operate on a 'patch system' such that an activity needs to be within their 'patch' in order for them to attend. A main road, a railway line, a building complex will in themselves be sufficient to act as a boundary to them. The low-key building of relationships is of vital importance in an area where tower blocks, main roads, and new developments cut individuals off from one another, and where the Church has traditionally been seen as the establishment – as 'them' bearing no relation to 'us'.

Integration of the Church and Its Mission to Children

Having considered its relationship to children and parents, it is essential that the Church reappraises its own approach towards its work with children, particularly in the area of Christian education.

Given the fact that the future of the Church lies in its youth and children, it is disturbing to observe the total lack of integration between adult members and children which is to be found in many congregations. Adults frequently express concern over the lack of young people in the adult services and the loss of children from the Sunday school as they reach teenage years. Yet children are virtually treated as second-class citizens in many situations. There is a sense in which work amongst children is seen by other sections of the Church as a rather minor adjunct to the real task of the Church in caring for adults. Hence, in some schools it is difficult to obtain sufficient staff with the necessary commitment and adequate time for lesson preparation. In certain churches, Sunday school is held at a different time from the regular Sunday worship and children are scarcely aware that an 'adult congregation' exists. In other churches there is a monthly family service, or children may join the adults for the first part of the 'adult service', but often this tends towards tokenism rather than meaningful interaction. Children are 'observers at' rather than 'participants in' worship. Many adults find their presence disturbing and feel that it is only when the children leave that the 'real' service can commence. Yet children can worship as well as adults, given guidance and understanding, and they should not be separated from this most important activity of the church family. Generally it happens that Sunday school becomes too young for the children, and many churches are unable to make provision for any intermediate grouping, neither are they able to adapt the adult service to the needs or culture of modern youth. Lacking a sense of belonging, youngsters soon lose interest and leave.

It is perhaps understandable that adult members of the congregation should find children somewhat disturbing. This is particularly so as many inner city churches find they are principally exercising a geriatric ministry in that the majority of their congregation is elderly, having grown up in a very different society from that of the present day. What many adult churchgoers regard as Christian virtues – obedience, quietness, sitting still, paying constant attention – are the exception rather than the rule amongst many children. In the inner city where 'nicking' or stealing is not uncommon, where telling the truth is not a priority, and where friendship is described as not 'grassing' on a mate to the police, it is small wonder that parts of the adult Christian community have difficulties in relating to such youngsters. Those working with the children have themselves to rethink and re-evaluate their approach and their own biases if they are seriously hoping to have any lasting influence on the children.

Ultimately, the most important aspect in the integration of the church and the Sunday school or any Christian mission with children, is that the child is aware of a sense of belonging and of acceptance by all. He needs to be wanted, appreciated and loved, he needs to know that he is sharing in the way things are done, he needs to feel that he has a part to play, and he needs to be given responsibility. Above all, he needs to know that he is a vital part of the Christian community. It is an approach such as this which will help to counteract the negative factors of boredom, loneliness, and non-acceptance which many youngsters, black and white, face in the inner city. Taken to its logical conclusion, it is not unrealistic to say that the majority of content teaching in the Sunday school or junior church could be sacrificed for the sake of making a child know he is accepted and of value as an individual.

Conclusion

In its response to children, the Church's aim is to share with them the love of God. Ultimately, it is only as they see this love in action, when Christians take the time and effort to build up relationships with them, that they will begin to respond in return. Children are not reached through talking and reasoning. They are reached through seeing that Christians love and care for them. Such caring is the basis of any form of evangelism amongst children and builds the bridgeheads which earn the Church a right to the hearing of the gospel. This is especially important in the inner city where many children lack care and love. Christians thus need constantly to re-examine their aims, attitudes, and methods in order to ensure that their message is being communicated as effectively as possible. This can only be achieved through the discipline of a periodic re-evaluation of the major elements in their work with children, putting themselves in the child's place.

NOTES

1 Charles Booth, *The Life and Labour of the People in London* (Macmillan, 1902), vol. vii, pp. 44–5.
2 *Samples from English Culture*, 1965.

Christian Education:
Kerygma *v.* Didache – Perspectives on the Future in the U.S.A.

John H. Westerhoff

Time, wrote St Augustine, is a threefold present: the present as we experience it, the past as present memory, and the future as present expectation. Each of us lives within the limits of our particular present; each of us needs to break free from the parochialisms by which we have a propensity to live. I need to acknowledge that I am an Episcopal priest, educated at Harvard and Columbia Universities, long identified with the progressive education movement in the tradition of Horace Bushnell and George Albert Coe and characterized as a liberal, socially and theologically. While I do not fully accept these labels, they may be helpful to the reader who wants to be free of my unavoidable prejudicial perspective.

To say that the issue facing Christian education in the United States is preaching *v.* teaching, as the title of this essay assumes, is perhaps a bit dramatic; it is certainly a caricature, but I think true. Historically the evangelical concern for proclamation, the religion of the heart, conversion and 'new birth' has been contrasted with the catechetical concern for instruction, the religion of the head, nurture, and 'growing-up'. In one sense it is a false dichotomy. At its best Christian educational theory in the United States affirmed both the transformation and the formation of the whole person. But practically these two modes of learning have been estranged and now have returned to plague those who are concerned about the educational ministry of the Church. The future will be shaped by how this issue is addressed. To understand fully the problem and its present manifestation we need to explore the history of the Sunday school in the United States.

While the early days of the Sunday school in the United States is best understood as an aspect of the charity movement and the means by which general education was provided for the poor, the common school movement, at the beginning of the nineteenth century, assumed this responsibility and the Sunday school early assumed the responsibility of winning and holding the new nation for evangelical Protestantism. In a few short years this lay, voluntary movement of Evangelical women and men became one of the most significant endeavours in this nation's history. Within the ecology of those Church-related institutions which emerged at the turn of the nineteenth century, the Sunday school is best understood primarily as an agency of evangelism. The Reverend William Hamill, Superintendent of Teacher Training for the Methodist Episcopal Church in the South, put it succinctly when he wrote:

> Everything we do in the Sunday school is but a means to an end . . . . The Sunday school has only one mighty and ever present purpose, and that is to win souls . . . . The Sunday school teacher utterly fails if he is not making spiritual impressions upon the boys and girls and turning their hearts and minds away from the follies and sins of human nature by the pure spirit and the transforming power of the gospel of God.[1]

Benjamin Jacobs, the Baptist layman who helped to transform the Sunday school into a world-wide movement, spoke of teaching as leading others, by example, on the road to spiritual maturity.[2] Children, he pointed out, may or may not study their Bibles as diligently as desired, but they will study the lives of the adults they meet in the church. Teachers, therefore, must be models of what they desire others to become; they are to be spiritual mentors, not instructors.

In 1887 John Vincent wrote *The Modern Sunday School.*

> The Sunday school is a modern title for an ancient and apostolic service of the Church. It is a school first and foremost for disciples. It is a school with a master, the teacher, and with his disciples gathered around him.[3]

Vincent, in this little book, presents a variety of roles a teacher might play: he can entertain his pupils and keep them happy; he can work at winning their admiration; he can make them into good scholars who know the Bible and the Church's doctrines. Vincent accepts none of these. Instead, he lists the spiritual qualities needed by a teacher so that he may aid in the spiritual conversion of those he meets. A number of years later Senabaugh wrote in a similar vein:

> Surely not just anyone can teach, for religion is caught more than taught and we cannot teach what we do not know. Religion is an experience and we cannot fully teach anything that we have not

verified. The teacher may teach about Christianity but if he is to teach Christ he must live in fellowship with him.[4]

In 1816 J. A. James wrote *The Sunday School Teacher's Guide*. He opened with a conviction:

> Teaching religion is something more than giving instruction. The accumulation of biblical facts and figures and the memorization of passages of Scripture are an insignificant part of religious training . . . Teaching is not to be an end in itself, but a means to and end, and that end that we seek is new life. . . .[5]

As late as 1920 Bernard W. Spilman, field secretary for the Southern Baptist Sunday School Board, wrote a popular book entitled *A Study of Religious Pedagogy*. The book was based on Jesus' encounter with the Samaritan woman at the well, a paradigm of conversion in the New Testament and a model for the Sunday school. Spilman makes it very clear that he believes that Christian education is of the heart, not the head and that teaching is not for moral guidance, but to save persons from sin. 'The aim of every Sunday School teacher', he wrote, 'should be to teach the message of salvation that the pupil, young and old, good and bad, shall see Jesus and seeing him receive forgiveness full and free.'[6]

But the North American scene was changing. A joke best characterizes that change. It began with a question. 'When is a school not a school?' The answer: 'When it is a Sunday School!' Some, mostly those in the established, white Anglo-Saxon mainline Protestant churches thought this to be a sick joke. In response to its scathing humour, they endeavoured to turn the Sunday school into a lavish educational institution, that is one modelled after the best of public schools, a *real school*, consistent with modern psychology and pedagogy. There were those who feared the results of these changes. In 1905 John Vincent, the great Methodist leader of the Sunday-school movement, then in his later years, gave an address at the Eleventh International Sunday School Convention in Toronto, Canada. He entitled his address, 'A Forward Look For the Sunday School'. Vincent began by saying he was going 'to dream of things that are to be'.[7] However, before he revealed his dream, he gave a warning:

> It is possible in our day to make too much of method, of recent educational theories, of curricula, and merely intellectual training.

The Sunday school in its desire to gratify modern educators is in danger of making a blunder and of sacrificing good things that are old. . . .[8]

Nevertheless, change was in the air. Teaching now became the dominant concern of Christian education, at least among most Presbyterians, Congregationalists, Methodists, Episcopalians, and other mainstream Christians. Since these folk represented both 'standard brand' Protestantism and the religious educational establishment, commentators have typically described their efforts as if they were normative. It is important to realize that this was not the case, but more of that later.

The Sunday school soon changed its name to the church school. Instead of seeking to convert persons, the school was, through instruction, to nurture persons gradually to Christian maturity. A new body of professionals, directors of religious education, were educated to direct church schools once led by lay Sunday-school superintendents and to train church-school teachers to engage in contemporary methods of instruction and use the newly published 'educationally sound' curriculum resources founded upon insights of child development. As Nevin Harner, a professor of Christian Education at a Reformed Church Seminary in 1932 wrote: 'Religious education must become a science in order to command the allegiance and the intellectual respect of an educated constituency.'[9]

Behind all these church-school endeavours was the conviction that '. . . a child is to grow up a Christian and never know himself as being otherwise',[10] a conviction which assumed that children could pass through a graded evolutionary process towards Christian maturity, or as George Albert Coe, the most significant voice in the modern religious education movement put it: '. . . instruction and training [should replace] evangelism'.[11] The President of the Hartford School of Religious Pedagogy, William Douglas MacKenzie, put it succinctly when he wrote: 'The fact that the Sunday-school teacher has for his supreme aim the bringing of the children to God must not obscure the fact that the means for doing so is not by direct evangelistic preaching, but by the *teaching* of the Bible.'[12] Even the demise of liberalism and the emergence of a post-liberal theology (the North American form of neo-orthodoxy) did not significantly affect the church school's emphasis on teaching. While the debate raged between those who wanted to emphasize nurture (socialization) and those who advocated instruction, none lost faith in the ability of the church school and the ministry of 'teaching' to educate Christians and to aid in their growth to maturity. Ellis Nelson in 1973 wrote '. . . the particular role of [Christian] education is to foster deliberate effort to help persons in the church develop a Christian mentality.'[13]

For the past two decades I have been associated with these efforts at teaching understood as nurture in Christian faith. The dilemma I faced was the apparent inadequacy of the church school for this task. Indeed, I was among those who were predicting the death of the church school. Then I read Robert Lynn's and Elliott Wright's history of the Sunday school, *The Big Little School*. It is Lynn's thesis that the Sunday school cannot be understood except in terms of nineteenth-century evangelical Protestantism. Further, I discovered that where that evangelical spirit is alive today, the Sunday school is prospering; note the growth of the Sunday school in 'fringe sects' such as the Church of the Nazarene and the Assembly of God denominations. Where that evangelical spirit is in decline, namely in most mainline denominations today, the church school is losing enrolment.

Throughout the southern states the old Sunday school with its emphasis on evangelism is growing. The ten largest Sunday schools in the United States – ranging from 2,500 to 8,000 weekly attendance – are related to the Southern Baptist Convention. Year after year, these congregations have accounted for 400 to 2,000 converts through their Sunday schools. For these evangelical churches, the Sunday school is considered the major mode of outreach for the Church. Within the Sunday school persons are converted and equipped to be evangelists. With 'soul winning' as their primary aim, 300 to 600 lay persons witness (teach) each Sunday and make between 500 to 1500 calls on their 'students' each week so as to testify to their conversion. While these Sunday schools are still led primarily by lay persons, the pastor is very much involved in what is best described as a congregational goal to 'teach for decision'.

It appears that these churches know how to convert others to Chirstian faith. However, they do not appear to know how to help persons grow up in the faith. Our mainline churches know a great deal more about helping persons grow up, but they do not seem to know how to convert anyone. Our evangelical churches know what it means to proclaim the gospel, our mainline churches know what it means to nurture persons in the gospel. They obviously need each other, but they are estranged. It wasn't always so. Recently I celebrated the Eucharist at a small Episcopal parish in North Carolina. It was built next to a cotton mill by the owner of the mill at the turn of the century. The owner of the mill then required his workers to attend the Sunday school in this church. Here he hoped they would be converted and thereby seek baptism and entrance into the liturgical life of the parish through which he assumed they were to be nurtured in the faith. But such understandings no longer exist and a once vital and growing Episcopal parish is now struggling for survival while the Baptist church down the street grows by leaps and bounds.

Today, as we enter the decade of the 1980s, we find Christian education in the United States in a demoralized state among mainline Protestants and in a confused state among evangelical Protestants. Mainline Protestants are beginning to ask questions about evangelism, proclamation, and conversion.[14] Evangelical Protestants, now near their option for growth, have 'come of age' and are questioning their need for catechesis, teaching, and nurture.[15] It is a time of uncertainty, a time of crises. How the future will be shaped is not clear, though one thing seems certain. The one-time estrangement of kerygma and didache has paid a tremendous price among both evangelicals and mainstream Protestants. A new understanding of their place in the church's ministry is beginning to be explored. Still the picture is blurred and little serious work has been done. I, therefore, must confess my scepticism about venturing any clear picture of our future. It is a murky picture at best. I am too close to it to achieve clarity; a variety of diverse voices abound. I have chosen, therefore, to describe my own thoughts on the educational ministry of the Church.

Evangelization and Catechesis

Since the turn of the century education in liberal, mainline Protestant churches has employed the language of nurture and avoided the issue of conversion. The gradual formation of Christians by home and church has provided the norm for our ministry. Nurture or socialization has informed our understandings and ways.[16] The aim of Christian education was to introduce persons into the life and mission of the community of Christian faith. Few of us have seriously questioned whether or not nurture provides both a sufficient and necessary category for Christian life. I want to affirm the necessity of nurture or catechesis, that process by which persons are socialized with a Christian community of faith.[17]

Catechesis is essentially a pastoral activity, including every aspect of the Church's life, intended to incorporate persons into the life of an ever-changing (reforming) tradition-bearing (catholic) community of Christian faith. It is a process intended to both recall and reconstruct the Church's tradition so that it might become conscious and active in the lives of maturing persons and communities. It is the process by which persons learn to understand, internalize, and apply the Christian revelation in daily individual and corporate life. As such, catechesis aims to enable the faithful to meet the two-fold responsibility which Christian faith asks of them: community with God and neighbour. Catechesis, therefore, is a life's work shared by all those who participate in the mission and ministry of the Christian Church. It values the interaction of faithing souls in community, striving to be faithful in-but-not-of-the-world. The fundamental question which catechesis asks is this: What is it to be Christian together in community and in the world? To answer this question is to understand the means by which we grow up as Christians within a community of faith. As such, catechesis occurs wherever divine revelation is made known, faith is enhanced and enlivened, or the vocation of persons is realized. Catechesis intends to aid us to understand the implication of Christian faith for life and our lives, to evaluate critically every aspect of our individual and corporate understandings and ways, and to become equipped and inspired for faithful activity in Church and society.

Importantly, catechesis acknowledges that we are socialized within a nurturing community.[18] Baptism incorporates us into a family with a living tradition. Branded with the sign of the cross and with a new surname, 'Christian', we are adopted into and destined to grow up in this new family. We are historical beings, implicitly and explicitly influenced and formed by the communities in which we live and grow. Catechesis acknowledges this influence and challenges all persons to be morally responsible for both the ways in which they live in community and for the ways by which they influence the lives of others. While catechesis affirms that persons are both determined and free, the product of nurture and the agent of nurture, it makes it incumbent upon the community of faith to accept responsibility for disciplined, intentional, faithful, obedient life together. Still, we cannot afford to believe that nurture or catechesis alone provides an adequate understanding of the Church's ministry.[19] Without evangelization and conversion, catechesis and nurture are inadequate.

Few concepts are more vague and confusing to liberal mainline Protestants than evangelization and conversion. Rarely have we used the word conversion, and all too frequently, evangelism has referred solely to membership campaigns. However, until we find a place for evangelization and conversion within our educational ministry, the Church's educational mission will remain impotent. Indeed, without converts, the Church will have difficulty being a community of Christian nurture.

Evangelization, as I am using the word, refers to the process by which the Christian community of faith, through the proclamation of the gospel in word and deed, leads persons inside the Church to a radical reorientation of life – conversion. Evangelization is not indoctrination. It is testifying through transformed lives to the acts of God both within and without the community of faith. When we evangelize we witness through word-in-deed to the acts of God in Jesus Christ. Without this personal living witness to the Lordship of Christ, to the good news of God's new possibility and to the gospel's prophetic protest against all false religiosity, the Church loses its soul and becomes an institution of cultural change living in and for God's coming community. Evangelization is best understood, therefore, as the means by which the Church continually transforms its life and the lives of its people into a body of committed believers, willing to give anything and everything to the cause of historically mediating God's reconciling love in the world.[20]

Christian faith goes counter to many ordinary understandings and ways of life. It is hardly possible for anything less than a converted, disciplined body to be the historical agent of God's work in the world. Christians are not made or formed through nurture. Conversions – reorientations of life, changes of heart, mind and behaviour – are a necessary aspect of mature Christian faith whether or not one grows up in the Church.

The Church can no longer surrender to the illusion that child nurture, in and of itself, can or will rekindle the fire of Christian faith either in persons or in the Church. We have expected too much of nurture. We can nurture persons into institutional religion, but not into mature Christian faith. The Christian faith by its very nature demands conversions. We do not gradually educate persons to be Christian. To be Christian is to be baptized into the community of the faithful, but to be a mature Christian calls for numerous experiences of conversion.

Conversion implies the reordering of our perceptions, a radical change without which no further growth or learning is possible. Conversion, therefore, is not an end, but a new beginning. It is a reorientation of a person's life, a deliberate turning from indifference, indecision, doubt, or earlier forms of piety to enthusiasm, conviction, illumination, and 'new' understandings and ways.[21]

Conversions make possible not only seeing anew that which past learning may have blocked, but seeing for the first time that which had been overlooked. A paradigm for this understanding of conversion is perhaps best seen in the life of Helen Keller. As a young child she had been sickened by a disease which left her unable to speak. Until the age of seven she existed much like an animal. Then her parents employed Anne Sullivan and after much frustration, one day in 1887, she experienced a conversion, a transformation in which she apprehended the meaning of a word and established a communication with the world and a means to relate to other persons previously impossible. In her autobiography she explains it this way:

We walked down the path of the well-house, attracted by the fragrance of the honeysuckle with which it was covered. Someone was drawing water and my teacher placed my hand under the spout. As the cool stream gushed over one hand she spelled into the other the word water, first slowly, then rapidly. I stood still, my whole attention fixed upon the motions of her fingers. Suddenly I felt a misty consciousness as of something forgotten – a thrill of returning thought; and somehow the mystery of language was revealed to me. I knew then that 'w-a-t-e-r' meant the wonderful cool something that was flowing over my hand. That living word awakened my soul, gave it light, hope, joy, set it free! There were barriers still, it is true, but barriers that could in time be swept away. I left the well-house eager to learn. Everything had a name, and each name gave birth to a new thought. As we returned to the house every object which I touched seemed to quiver with life. That was because I saw everything with the strange new sight that had come to me.[22]

Helen Keller's experience is that of a new birth in the world. The word WATER had been lost and was found. The word found gave her power to know beyond herself. It was a breakthrough, a moment of insight, a revelation.

At first glance this story may seem to have little to do with either our lives or the gospel narrative. Her experience seems so unique. We are not physically blind or deaf. Still, on another level, we do hear without understanding and see without perceiving. I contend that we cannot gradually educate persons to be Christians, not in this world. Christian faith goes counter to our ordinary understandings and ways. It is hardly possible to grow up in our sort of society and have the eyes and ears of Christian faith. Transformations, reorientations of life, conversions are necessary.

Of course talk of conversions leaves many liberal Christians feeling uneasy. They are reminded of revival tents, radio preachers, and militant evangelists. But before we too easily discount the importance of conversions consider this story.

> A priest was studying for his doctorate at Marquette University where the teachings of the eminent Jesuit Roman Catholic Scholar Bernard Lonergan prevailed. On this occasion, the priest, a disciple of Lonergan's rigid theological method, was entertaining Wolfhard Pannenberg, an equally eminent Protestant systematic theologian, who teaches at the University of Munich. 'Who is your principal mentor?' asked Pannenberg. 'Lonergan', the priest replied. 'What a pity', remarked Pannenberg, 'he is nothing but a pietist.'[23]

Now a pietist is one who bases beliefs on inner feelings and often a good bit on anti-intellectualism. What could Pannenberg have meant by this put-down? Lonergan's theological method, as rigorous as it is, holds that, before a person can move from Scripture and tradition, that is from what has been said about God by others, and construct a theology for himself there has to be a conversion. Conversion in this case is best understood as a falling in love and a subsequent opening of the eyes and ears to that which lies beyond the boundaries of our common and usual experience and knowing. Faith, maintains Lonergan, cannot be grounded in reason alone. Pannenberg, on the other hand, is committed to the grounding of faith in reason alone and is therefore opposed to any appeal to conversion. I contend that Lonergan is correct.

Conversion is not solely a shift from no faith or another faith to Christian faith; it is also an essential dimension in the life of all baptized, faithful, Christians. Those who have been baptized as children and reared in the Church need to be converted. At various points every Christian must internalize the faith of the Church and affirm that faith as his own. At various points all Christians must examine the faith they claim and the lives they live, resolving the dissonance between possibility and reality by radical changes and new commitments.

Authentic Christian life is personal and social life lived on behalf of God's reign in the political, social, economic world. One cannot be nurtured into such life – not in this world. Every culture strives to socialize persons to live in harmony with life as it is. The culture calls upon its religious institutions to bless the *status quo* and it calls upon religion's educational institutions to nurture persons into an acceptance of life as it is.

But God calls his/her people to be signs of Shalom, the vanguard of God's Kingdom, a community of cultural change. To live in the conviction that such counter-cultural life is our Christian vocation in-but-not-of-the-world, necessitates conversions as well as nurture.

Once again we need to understand that both evangelization and catechesis have a place in the Church's ministry if it is to be Christian. Our sole concern for nurture has contributed to our losing both an evangelical power and a social dynamic. While rejecting a sterile revivalism, we constructed a false evangelism through nurture. True evangelization means helping persons to see that they are called not only to believe the Church's affirmation that Jesus is the Christ, to accept the fact of the resurrection, but to commit their lives to him and to live as his apostles (witnesses) in the world, to have faith in the resurrection.

Who but the converted can adequately nurture? And who but the nurtured can be adequately prepared for the radicalness of transformed life? Without the witness of Word-in-deed, which is the evangelical act, conversion cannot occur. Without nurture the converted cannot adequately bear witness in the world. Unless conversion and nurture are united in the Church's ministry, the Church will have difficulty being the Church of Jesus Christ, the bearer of the gospel in the world.

Evangelization involves the proclamation of the gospel which leads to ever-increasing and maturing commitments of faith.

Catechesis involves the process of making this ever-deepening faith become living, conscious, and active in the person.

Children, youth, and adults can and do make commitments of faith. Each new commitment, appropriate to the age and development of the person, provides a basis for reflection, understanding, and assimilation. Thus growth in faith develops over a lifetime: through evangelization the gospel is proclaimed and explained; through catechesis faith is enhanced and enlivened.

What the Church's ministry needs is a catechesis which evangelizes and evangelization which catechizes. Nurture and conversion, conversion and nurture, belong together taking different shapes and forms at various moments in a person's faith pilgrimage within the faith community.

Catechesis focuses on spiritual formation and the nurture of persons within a community of faith which through its pastoral ministry makes divine revelation known, enhances and enlivens faith, and aids persons in the realization of their vocation. Evangelization focuses on spiritual transformation and the conversions of persons within a community of faith which through its pastoral ministry bears prophetic witness in word and deed to the presence of God's Word in history.

Evangelization proclaims and explains the gospel so that faith might be aroused. Catechesis makes possible the growth and development of faith. The process is never-ending. Evangelization and catechesis, conversion and nurture belong together. Each is necessary for the other; when they are estranged the Church fails in its ministry and neglects its mission. Today it is incumbent upon us to affirm the necessary paradox of catechesis and evangelization within the Church and to reinterpret the nature and means of nurture and conversion within a community of faith. To the degree that we are successful, the Christian Church will be faithful.

The praxis of Christian life is a continual movement from nurture to conversion to nurture to conversion to nurture throughout a lifetime, in ways peculiar and appropriate to various stages in one's life. Growth in faith involves a continual reminder of our true human condition; we need to acknowledge that we are a justified, saved, redeemed people. Through significant experiences we also need to be made aware of our denied potential, our lack of fulfilment, and the dissonance between who we really are and how we live. Jarred loose from our complacency we need the time and space to mull over and wrestle with our dissonances until we come to a new cognitive, affective or volitional. Once that is accomplished, we need to assimilate and understand their implication for our lives. The first two steps are best understood as conversion through evangelization and the latter two as nurture through catechesis. Nevertheless, it is a never-ending process as we 'work out our salvation' day by day.

The Future of Christian Education

It appears that until we bring evangelization and catechesis together in our educational ministry it will be less than effective. My model for a future church school is therefore more like the earlier Sunday school than our contemporary church school. Until aspects of the old Sunday school are reintroduced, the Church will lack a necessary dynamic for life in a secular world.

Once I visited a number of small pure Hawaiian churches. They still called their church schools Sunday schools, though through the years they had obediently and faithfully tried to develop a Christian education programme like those recommended by the Church's educational professionals. They struggled to raise money to build classrooms; they bought the denominational curriculum and sent their people to teacher training workshops and lab schools. Still, attendance dropped, teachers were difficult to secure, and more seriously the faith was not adequately transmitted. They asked me why they were failing. I was stumped. They were doing everything we had suggested, yet they were unsuccessful. In desperation I asked them to tell me about the days when they were succeeding. And they did. They explained how many of their churches used to gather each Sunday afternoon for a *luau*. Young and old came together to dramatize Bible stories, sing hymns, testify and witness to their faith, eat and have fellowship together. They did almost everything natural to their culture except dance; we taught them that was immoral. When they finished describing their old Sunday school, I suggested they return to having *luaus*.

The old Sunday school appears to have cared most about creating an environment where people can be religious together, where persons can experience Christian faith and see it witnessed to in the words and deeds of significant others. The old Sunday school seemed to be aware of the importance of the affections, of story telling, of experience, of proclamation, and of role models. While many of these concerns remain in the rhetoric of the modern church school movement, we seem to have created an institution more concerned with teaching strategies, instructional gimmicks, and curricular resources than spiritual mentors; more concerned with age-graded classes for cognitive growth than communities concerned with the affections, more concerned with the goals of knowing about the Bible, theology, and Church history than communities experiencing and acting upon the faith.

That may be unfair to the modern church school and a fiction of the old Sunday school, but I think that most of us in our mainline churches are aware of how little of the story we know and how empty our moral and spiritual lives have become.

The future of Christian education in liberal mainline denominational churches will be in the creation of new-old intergenerational Sunday schools where persons will gather to witness through word-and-deed to the Christian story and way of life as their story and way of life.

Other modes and contexts for nurture and catechesis, such as the Sunday liturgy, retreats, action-reflection groups, will be necessary. But a Sunday church school with a focus on evangelization complimented by catechesis within the liturgical life of the congregation is possible and necessary. What such endeavours will look like is still within the imagination. Their realization remains the challenge confronting the future of Christian education in the United States.

And so I close by quoting the words of John Vincent, who wrote more than a century after the founding of the first Sunday school and more than a century ago:

> In the interest of the Church, the home, the state and society, we who represent this Sunday school sing with Robert Browning our song of hope:
> 'The best is yet to be,
> The last of life, for which the first was made.'[24]

NOTES

1 H. M. Hamill, 'The Sunday School as an Educational Force' in *The Development of the Sunday School 1780–1905* (Boston, The International Sunday School Associates, 1905), p. 176.

2 See: John Westerhoff, 'Models of Teaching for Religious Faith', *The Religious Educator*, September 1974.

3 John Vincent, *The Modern Sunday School* (New York, Hunt and Eaton, 1887), p. 32.

4 L. F. Senabaugh, *The Small Church School* (Nashville, Tenn., Cokesbury, 1930), p. 39.

5 J. A. James, *The Sunday School Teacher's Guide* (New York, The Female Union Society for the Growth of Sabbath Schools, 1816), pp. 83–4.

6 Bernard U. Spilman, *A Study of Religious Pedagogy* (New York, Fleming H. Revell and Company, 1920), p. 28.

7 John Vincent, 'A Forward Look for the Sunday School' in *The Eleventh International Sunday School Convention* (Boston, Mass., Executive Committee of International Sunday School Assn., 1905), p. 166.

8 Ibid., p. 166.

9 Nevin Harner, 'Is Religious Education to Become a Science?' in *Religious Education*, vol. xxvii (March 1932), p. 205.

10 Horace Bushnell, *Christian Nurture* (New Haven, Yale University Press, 1846), p. 4.

11 George Albert Coe, *A Social Theory of Religious Education* (New York, Scribners, 1917), p. 337.

12 William D. Mackenzie, 'The Relation of the Sunday School to the Art of Teaching' in *The Development of the Sunday School 1780–1905* (Boston, The International Sunday School Association, 1905), p. 178.

13 C. Ellis Nelson, 'Is Christian Education Something Particular?' in *Religious Education*, vol. lxvii (January–February 1972), p. 13.

14 See: John Westerhoff, *Will Our Children Have Faith?* (New York, Seabury, 1976) and 'Christian Initiation: Conversion and Nurture' in *Learning Through Liturgy* (New York, Seabury, 1978).

15 See: Lawrence Richards, *A Theology of Christian Education* (Grand Rapids: Zondervon, 1975).

16 Three significant works on Christian nurture are: Roger L. Shinn, *The Educational Mission of Our Church*, Philadelphia, United Church Press, 1962; Randolph Crump Miller, *Christian Nurture and the Church*, New York, Charles Scribner's Sons, 1961; and C. Ellis Nelson, *Where Faith Begins*, Richmond, Virginia, John Knox Press, 1967.

17 Important historic works which emphasize nurture are: Horace Bushnell, *Christian Nurture*, New Haven, Yale University Press, 1916; and George Albert Coe, *A Social Theory of Religious Education*, New York, Scribners, 1917.

18 The work of Bernard Marthler at Catholic University is most important for understanding catechesis. In particular see: Bernard Marthler, *Catechetics in Context*, Huntingdon, Indiana, Our Sunday Visitor, 1973. Also see John Westerhoff and Gwen Kennedy Neville, *Generation to Generation*, Philadelphia, Pilgrim Press, 1972.

19 See Johannes Hofinger, *Evangelization and Catechesis*. New York, Paulist Press, 1976.

20 See Alfred Krass, *Beyond the Either-or Church*, Nashville, Tidings, 1973, and Gabriel Fackre, *Do and Tell: Engagement Evangelism in the '70's*, Grand Rapids, Eerdmans Publishing Company, 1973.

21 Conversion is a topic which deserves more serious attention than it has been given. See especially Arthur Darby Nock, *Conversion*, New York, Oxford, 1961.

22 Helen Keller, *The Story of My Life* (Garden City, New York, 1904), pp. 23-4.

23 See John Westerhoff, *Will Our Children Have Faith?*, New York, Seabury, 1978, and *Bringing Up Children in the Christian Faith*, Minneapolis, Minn., Winston, 1980.

24 John Vincent, 'A Forward Look for the Sunday School', op. cit., p. 164.

Index

Index